T3-BNM-704

EXEMPLARY LIVES: SELECTED SERMONS ON THE SAINTS, FROM RHEINAU

Edited and Translated, with an Introduction,

by James C. Wilkinson

MARQUETTE
UNIVERSITY

PRESS

REFORMATION TEXTS WITH TRANSLATION (1350-1650)

Kenneth Hagen, General Editor

Theology and Piety, Vol. 3
Ian Levy, Editor

Production and cover: Joan Skocir.

Cover graphic from Ms Rh 052 f79, by permission of the Zürich Zentralbibliothek. See page 3.

Library of Congress Cataloging-in-Publication Data

Rheinauer Predigtsammlung. English & Middle High German. Selections.
 Exemplary lives : selected sermons on the saints, from Rheinau /
edited and translated, with an introduction, by James C. Wilkinson.
  p. cm. — (Reformation texts with translation (1350-1650). Series
Theology and piety ; v. 3)
  Includes bibliographical references (p.   ) and indexes.
  ISBN-13: 978-0-87462-709-1 (pbk. : alk. paper)
  ISBN-10: 0-87462-709-5 (pbk. : alk. paper)
  1. Christian saints—Sermons. 2. Christian saints. 3. Sermons, German.
 I. Wilkinson, James C. (James Christopher), 1954-   . II. Title. III.
Series: Reformation texts with translation (1350-1650). Theology and
piety ; v 3.
  BX880.R47 2006
  282.092'2—dc22
  [B]   2006002968

© 2006 Marquette University Press
Milwaukee, Wisconsin 53201-3141
All rights reserved.
www.marquette.edu/mupress/

♾The paper used in this publication meets the minimum requirements of the
American National Standard for Information Sciences—
Permanence of Paper for Printed Library Materials, ANSI Z39.48-1992.

Association of American
University Presses

MARQUETTE UNIVERSITY PRESS
MILWAUKEE

The Association of Jesuit University Presses

CONTENTS

Our thanks to Dr. Christoph Eggenberger, Curator of Manuscripts at the Zürich Zentralbibliothek for locating Ms Rh 052 f79 for the cover and to Dr. Petrus Tax for providing it to this publication.

Preface

James C. Wilkinson's volume of fifteenth-century sermons marks the third volume in the *Theology and Piety* series within *Reformation Texts with Translation (1350-1650)*. The previous two volumes offered material from the sixteenth century, both products of 'reform,' be it the efforts on the Roman side in the work of Cardinal Contarini, or those of the Lutheran Urbanus Rhegius. Here Dr. Wilkinson gives us a valuable look at the beliefs and devotional practices of the monks of Rheinau and the lay people who came to hear their sermons. This volume reminds us that for the vast majority of people on the eve of the Reformation, the Christian faith could not be boiled down to a set of scholastic propositions about the soteriological process, the various categories and subcategories of faith and grace, which had been worked out in the universities. Here, in the dialect of the local farmers and craftsmen, and free from all the looming controversies, were stories that spoke of faithful saints, pious deeds, and a loving God. If we are to understand the Reformation properly, we must gain a deeper understanding of the whole world from which it was born; Dr. Wilkinson's volume will prove to be of much assistance in that endeavor. This volume represents the sort of solid and meticulous scholarship which is indispensable for serious study of the period – a close reading, transcription, and translation of medieval manuscripts. It is the product of many years of hard work. Unfortunately, just as the project was nearing its completion, when the great bulk of the work had been done, Dr. Wilkinson grew gravely ill and could no longer continue. Thankfully, his mentor, Professor Petrus Tax, was kind enough to step in and take up the final editorial tasks essential to bringing this volume to completion. We, the editors, remain in Professors Tax's debt, and we extend every prayer to Dr. Wilkinson.

Dr. Ian Levy
Lexington Theological Seminary
Lexington, Kentucky

Foreword

The series "Reformation Texts With Translation (1350-1650)" appears as a welcome new initiative to make important scholarly texts of a religious or spiritual nature available to a public that is less conversant in foreign languages. The time span 1350-1650 casts a wide enough net to catch pre- as well as post-Reformation works of interest. And the volumes that have appeared clearly indicate that religious texts before, alongside, and even against the Reformation are considered. Nicholas of Lyra, for instance, died in 1349; his *Postilla on the Song of Songs*, which appeared as volume 3 in this series (1998), is still far from the Reformation and very much Christian in a medieval sense. On the other hand, Philipp Melanchthon's *Annotations on the First Epistle to the Corinthians* (volume 2 in the series, 1995) is clearly a work of the Reformation. But the volume *Convents Confront the Reformation: Catholic and Protestant Nuns in Germany* (1996) manifests in its title already some counterpositions; also, the works of two of these German nuns published in this volume were originally printed as late as 1658 (Anna Sophia, Abbess of Quedlinburg) and 1678 (Martha Elisabeth Zitter). Apparently, the editors welcome diversity, the new as well as the old, action and reaction. So do many readers.

In this spirit I am grateful to the editors of the series, Kenneth Hagen and Ian Levy, for their willingness to publish James C. Wilkinson's selection of German-Swiss sermons on the saints from the so-called *Rheinauer Predigtsammlung* (15th century). These sermons are in several ways special: They exhibit a great variety of simple Christian religiousness, trust in God and the saints, veneration of these saints, and belief in miracles and in the intercession with God or Christ which they effect for all kinds of sinners when asked, etc. Any later reformer could have easily lambasted or parodied any or all of these texts. But these sermons remain attractive: Their style is simple, matter-of-fact, and very much that of the spoken language of the time and area; they are short, the preacher is not dogmatic, but rather objective, also giving much attention to women and Jews. Also, the exemplum which usually fleshes out the second part of each sermon often exemplifies a special story, miracle, or intervention of a high narrative or even entertainment value. It is very likely that the audience of these brief, vernacular sermons consisted mainly of lay people, probably also of men and women working in the farms or on the land near Rheinau Abbey. Some readers may have a certain nostalgia for these sermons with their uncomplicated but genuine medieval Christian spirituality.

Many years ago, when I was teaching a course in German civilization (including the Middle Ages), an undergraduate student asked me in a very friendly way whether I would ever consider teaching my material from the point of view of the working man (perhaps the student was tired of hearing so much about the clergy and nobility of all ranks or about the liberal arts and the intelligensia). Of course, I had to tell him that we hardly had any reliable historical documentation about the "working classes" until the nineteenth century. Although the Rheinau sermons aren't strictly speaking historical source material, they nevertheless reflect in several ways how simple people of the late Middle Ages looked at, felt about, and especially lived their Christian and saint-centered religion. As mirrors of a pre-Reformation era of relatively uncomplicated but also unbroken interior as well as exterior religiousness, these sermons are still appealing and in a way precious.

Petrus W. Tax, Professor emeritus of German,
the University of North Carolina at Chapel Hill

This work is dedicated to my late father, James Everett Wilkinson, who early in my life impressed upon me the value of a job well done.

INTRODUCTION

Located on an island in the Rhine River in Switzerland, near Schaffhausen, Rheinau was the site of a Benedictine abbey with the original patrons St. Mary and St. Peter, and, at a later date, St. Catherine. Rheinau Abbey was founded around 780 A.D., with monastic activities of varying degrees of intensity continuing there until 1862. The abbey's scriptorium flourished in the twelfth century. On the other hand, a particularly low point came between 1529 and 1532, when the monks left Rheinau because of the Reformation. The monastery was taken over by the worldly authorities in 1862. Since 1867, Rheinau Abbey has been used as a psychiatric clinic.

THE MANUSCRIPT

In a fifteenth-century Swiss-German manuscript there is a collection of sermons associated with Rheinau entitled *Die Rheinauer Predigtsammlung*. This manuscript, consisting of paper rather than parchment, has been housed since the eighteenth century in the Central Library in Zürich under the signature C 102a.[1] The pages have a format of 21.0 by 14.5 cm. This Rheinau collection contains a total of eighty-three sermons which are divided into two sections: *De Tempore* is a collection of fifty-five sermons (pp. 1-295 in the original manuscript) on Sundays and mostly changeable feast days in the liturgical year, beginning with the first Sunday of Advent.[2] The second section, *De Sanctis*, contains twenty-eight sermons (pp. 297-490) on the lives of saints.[3]

1. A complete description of the Rheinau sermon collection can be found in Leo Cunibert Mohlberg, *Katalog der Handschriften der Zentralbibliothek Zürich* (Zürich: Buchdruckerei Berichthaus, 1952). Vol. 1, Mittelalterliche Handschriften, 53 and 360 (addition). The collection hasn't been discussed in the standard histories of the (medieval) German sermon (Wackernagel, Cruel, and even Schneyer).

2. Recently (1996), ten of these *De Tempore* sermons have been edited by Francesca Trigonella (with a valuable commentary), "Ausgewählte Predigten aus der Handschrift C 102 a der Zentralbibliothek Zürich. Text und Kommentar" (Lizentiatsarbeit, Universität Zürich, 1996).

3. See my 1988 dissertation for a complete edition of these 28 sermons with several analyses (language, structure, components, and content) in the Introduction. There are fragments of another, closely related version, a total of ten sermons, in the Benedictine monastery at Metten in Bavaria; see Michael Huber, "Homilienfragmente aus der Benediktinerstiftsbibliothek Metten," *Münchener Museum für Philologie des Mittelalters und der Renaissance* 1 (1911, rpt. 1972): 339-55. These fragments don't duplicate any of the sermons from the *De Sanctis* section of the Rheinau manuscript, but there are duplicates of some of the sermons from *De Tempore*.

It is not certain whether this manuscript was written at Rheinau Abbey; it may well have been written elsewhere,[4] yet the sermons touch on topics which would certainly have been of interest to the monastic community at this monastery as well as to other audiences in the neighborhood.

There is, however, nothing directly written in the Rheinau manuscript concerning the type of original audience who heard the sermons of the *Rheinauer Predigtsammlung*. The particular saints whose feast days are celebrated in the *De Sanctis* section of the Rheinau manuscript would be of interest to an audience of monks, nuns, lay brothers, and lay sisters. In addition to the patron saints at Rheinau, whose lives are dealt with in the collection of Rheinau sermons, there is also a sermon on St. Benedict, whose Rule was followed at the abbey. In line 8 of this sermon, St. Benedict is referred to as "our father." At least the preacher of this sermon was a Benedictine monk or priest. But since all sermons in the Rheinau manuscript exhibit the same style and "voice," this Benedictine preacher appears to be the overall (last) writer or "editor" of them.

J. Werner concludes that the sermons in the Rheinau manuscript were not even originally delivered in the abbey at Rheinau itself. He proposes in his 1926 article on the Rheinau sermon collection that someone from the abbey at Rheinau preached these sermons to a congregation of lay people in their village church.[5] Werner notes the preacher's reference to matters in the *De Tempore* section which by no means involve weighty theological topics, such as the preacher's remarks against those people who adhere to superstitious customs. Werner also notes that the topic of raising children is addressed in a passage in this *De Tempore* section in which the example of Jesus' obedience to his mother is emphasized.[6]

Yet it might well be the case that the Rheinau sermons were delivered at the abbey, and that the secular, mundane, or agrarian nature of some remarks in the sermons could then perhaps indicate that lay brothers and lay sisters were present there among the monks hearing the sermons at Rheinau. The saints treated in these sermons would clearly be inspirational role models for the monastic community in

---

4. Hans-Jochen Schiewer states definitively: "Die Hs. stammt nicht aus dem 1862 aufgehobenen Benediktinerstift Rheinau südl. von Schaffhausen..." in his entry concerning the *Rheinauer Predigtsammlung* in *Die deutsche Literatur des Mittelalters Verfasserlexikon*, ed. Kurt Ruh, vol. 8 (Berlin: Walter de Gruyter, 1992), col. 28.

5. J. Werner, "Volkskundliches aus einer Rheinauer Predigtsammlung des 15. Jahrhunderts," *Schweizerisches Archiv für Volkskunde* 26 (1926): 280.

6. J. Werner, "Volkskundliches aus einer Rheinauer Predigtsammlung des 15. Jahrhunderts," *Schweizerisches Archiv für Volkskunde* 26 (1926): 281.

and around the abbey at Rheinau. Yet there are also certain references in the saints' section of the Rheinau manuscript sermons which apparently address a more general audience, as Werner notes is also the case in the *De Tempore* section. Among these remarks in the saints' sermons are frequent reminders of the relevance of the saints' lives to the average person as a defense against the dangerous interventions of the devil into our lives. The hearers of the sermons are also warned about loquaciousness among women,[7] high spirits and gambling among young people,[8] and swearing.[9]

Despite the occasional negative remarks on women, and even though sermons on male saints outnumber those on female saints in the original manuscript, the representation of women among the saints honored in the *Rheinau Predigtsammlung* is by no means scant. There are four sermons in this Rheinau manuscript on feast days associated with St. Mary. Such a strong representation of St. Mary in the Rheinau collection may very well also reflect the general importance of the veneration of St. Mary during the Middle Ages. The fact that St. Mary was one of the original patron saints of the abbey certainly accounts, too, for the saint's strong presence in the *De Sanctis* section of the manuscript.

The sermon on St. Mary Magdalene effectively illustrates Christ's ability to raise mankind out of the darkest sin to a new life, accomplishing, in effect, a resurrection of the soul. The sermon on St. Catherine is one in which there is a strong emphasis on wisdom and learning, offering this saint as a strong role model for those in Rheinau Abbey engaged in intellectual pursuits.

Since the abbey most likely possessed several pieces of land in its neighborhood and certainly had several dependencies (chapels and churches) in areas around it, one can safely assume that these sermons were also preached to a wider audience of lay people on the feast days of these saints.[10] The simple, strongly oral style of these texts (uncomplicated syntax and imagery, lack of difficult and foreign words or theological terms) supports the idea of a quite unsophisticated audience. In addition to the simple religiousness and style of these sermons, a further strong argument for an audience of lay and even

---

7. This is referred to in the sermon on the Assumption of the Blessed Virgin St. Mary, ll. 20-23.

8. This is also in the sermon on the Assumption, ll. 85-104.

9. Sermon on the Assumption, ll. 106-108.

10. In the introduction to his edition of the Rheinau *Liber Ordinarius*, p. XLII-XLIII, A. Hänggi lists several churches and chapels that were built during the 12th century in the parishes that were dependent on Rheinau Abbey. It is not likely that this number decreased during the later Middle Ages.

working people is the brevity of these sermons. The average length is around a hundred fifty lines in the manuscript. Such a sermon can be preached in ten to fifteen minutes. Since the feasts of the saints regularly fall and are celebrated on weekdays, it makes much sense for the preacher to keep matters brief, so that the attending working people don't lose too much time. For sure, a few of the sermons are about 50 percent longer, as for instance the one on the Assumption of Mary (241 lines). But since Mary was one of the patron saints of Rheinau Abbey, there very likely was a procession during or following the service so that the worshipers were allowed to have more time off.

These saints' sermons show generally the same structure:

1. biblical citations are presented which either apply directly to the specific saint whose feast day is being celebrated, or verses which are allegorically interpreted in the preacher's text to apply to the saint;[11]

2. information on the life of the saint, in almost all cases, presenting events leading up to and including the saint's martyrdom;[12]

3. an exemplum, or as referred to in the German text, a *bischaft* or *mer*, an illustrative tale in which the saint him/herself often appears in order to bring about the salvation of the soul of the protagonist in the tale, such as in the *exempla* concerning Theophilius (ll. 116-238 in the sermon on the Assumption) or the bishop who held St. Andrew in great esteem[13] or, in one case, the resolution of a secular problem, that is, in the recovery of stolen money in the sermon on St. Nicholas;

4. a brief admonition to the congregation to call for the saint's aid in order to live righteously and eventually reach heaven in the beyond.

There are certain references to source materials within the texts of some Rheinauer saints' sermons. Jacobus da Voragine's *Legenda Aurea* is referred to in the original Rheinau text as the *Lambartik* (St. Thomas, l. 44) as well as the *Gulden Buoch* (St. Nicholas, l. 31).[14] The sermons also feature biblical citations (without chapter and verse specifically indicated) which I have identified and noted in the right margin of the transcribed manuscript pages on which they occur in this edition. Also in the pages of the original manuscript there are

11. See the sermon on the Annunciation to St. Mary, ll. 87-95.
12. The following saints featured in this edition did not suffer martyrdom: Sts. Nicholas, Mary (Candlemas, Annunciation, Assumption, Birth), Mary Magdalene, Benedict.
13. Both Theophilius and the bishop come very close to succumbing to the wiles of the devil.
14. Theodor Grässe, ed. *Jacobi a Voragine Legenda Aurea: Vulgo Historia Lombardica Dicta.* 1890, rpt. (Osnabrück: Zeller, 1969).

quotes of authoritative saints (Bernard of Clairvaux,[15] Gregory the Great,[16] John Chrysostom[17]). Most if not all of these quotes from authorities may have been incorrectly ascribed and thus could not be identified.[18] Information of a biographical nature on the saints was apparently taken, although not always in its entirety, from Jacobus da Voragine. Source material for the *exempla* of the sermons can be found in Jacobus' *Legenda Aurea*, as well as in the *Patrologia Latina* and the *Gesta Romanorum*.[19] Eugen Wolter[20] has collected the sources for the tale of the Jewish boy which appears in the sermon on Candlemas.[21]

The Rheinau *De Sanctis* section contains the following twenty-eight sermons: St. Andrew (Nov. 30), St. Nicholas (Dec. 6), St. Thomas (Dec. 21), St. Stephen (Dec. 26), St. John the Evangelist (Dec. 27), Candlemas (Feb. 2), St. Benedict (March 21), the Annunciation (March 25), St. Mark (April 25), Sts. Philip and James the Younger (May 1), the Finding of the Holy Cross (May 3), St. John the Baptist (June 24), Sts. Peter and Paul (June 29), St. Mary Magdalene (July 22), St. James the Elder (July 25), St. Lawrence (Aug. 10), the Assumption of St. Mary (Aug. 15), St. Bartholomew (Aug. 24), the Beheading of St. John the Baptist (Aug. 29), the Birth of St. Mary (Sept. 8), the Raising of the Holy Cross (Sept. 14), St. Matthew (Sept. 20), St. Michael (Sept. 29), Sts. Simon and Judas (Oct. 28), All Saints' (Nov. 1), All Souls' (Nov. 2), St. Martin (Nov. 11), and St. Catherine (Nov. 25). One sees clearly that this is a selection: about one tenth of the available three hundred saints' days within one year is covered; it also becomes manifest from the dates that the sequence simply follows the liturgical year, from the Advent to just before the next Advent. Also, apparently there are four sermons on the subject of St. Mary, the Mother of Jesus, alone; four sermons do not directly

15. Quoted in the sermon on All Saints' Day, ll. 77-81.
16. Quoted in the sermon on All Saints' Day, ll. 81-94.
17. Also quoted in the sermon on All Saints', ll. 126-29, as well as in the sermon on the Feast of the Visitation, ll. 258-64.
18. Since these quotes couldn't be identified, it isn't always clear where they end.
19. Edited by Hermann Oesterley, Berlin 1872.
20. Eugen Wolter, ed. *Der Judenknabe: 5 griechische, 14 lateinische und 8 französische Texte*. Bibliotheca Normannica, vol II (Halle: Niemeyer, 1879). A version of this exemplum can also be found in the *Legenda Aurea*, but Jacobus da Voragine lists it under his information on the Assumption of St. Mary.
21. It would take too much space to give references to all the sources, which the author of the Rheinau sermons might have used; see the introduction of my dissertation, pp. xlvi-clv, for the references and an extensive discussion.

describe the life of one particular saint: All Saints', All Souls', the Finding of the Cross, and the Raising of the Cross.

From these twenty-eight sermons I have selected fourteen for this edition and translation. I have of course included the Rheinau patron saints: St. Mary with three (out of four) of the more interesting sermons (Candlemas, the Annunciation, the Assumption), Sts. Peter and Paul, St. Catherine; I have also chosen two other apostles: St. Andrew and St. Thomas, and one evangelist: St. Mark; in addition, St. Stephen as the first martyr, St. Mary Magdalene as another woman very close to Christ; St. Benedict as the founder of the Benedictine order as well as St. Nicholas (for folkloristic reasons) also deserved to be included.

Even if the Rheinau collection of sermons wasn't compiled at Rheinau Abbey, the selection of saints' sermons offered in the original manuscript appears to have been made to correspond to the history of the abbey at Rheinau. Monastic activities at Rheinau were conducted according to the Benedictine Rule. There is a sermon in the Rheinau collection devoted to St. Benedict. When Rheinau Abbey was founded, its patron saints were St. Mary, Mother of God, and St. Peter. St. Mary is represented in the collection with sermons on Candlemas, the Assumption,[22] her Birth, and a sermon on the Annunciation, which (following Luke's Gospel) also includes some lines in reference to the Visitation.[23] There is a sermon on St. Peter, which also celebrates St. Paul, on June 29. St. Catherine, who later during the Middle Ages also became a patron saint of Rheinau Abbey, has a sermon in celebration of her feast as the last sermon of the Rheinau collection. The life of St. Catherine, one which emphasizes the importance of learning and of the intellect, might have been preached at Rheinau for the purpose of strengthening the monks' or nuns' intellectual endeavors.

As it is stated in §50 of the *Dogmatic Constitution on the Church*, "… we seek from the saints examples in their way of life, fellowship in their communion, and aid by their intercession." Those who listened to the saints' sermons from Rheinau were given accounts of these twenty-four saints' lives of heroic faith. The congregation is reminded of the beauty of the communion of saints. Upon the death of a saint,

22. In lines 49-51 of this sermon, St. Mary is described as "the greatest saint who was ever born and sanctified on earth." Note that in the last sermon of the *De Tempore* section (no. 55: On the dedication of the church) the preacher ends with, "… with this may help us God the Father and God the Son and God the Holy Spirit and she, <our> Advocate, the royal mother Mary, Amen"; see the original text in Francesca Trigonella, *Ausgewählte Predigten* …(1996): 57.

23. These are lines in the text, ll. 47-55, which augment the biblical account of Gabriel's annunciation to the Virgin St. Mary.

by natural causes as well as martyrdom, the immediate reward for the saints is the reunion with his/her brethren in the beyond. In the sermon for the feast day of St. Stephen, the preacher refers to the communion of saints as a blessed state.[24]

Although, as was noted previously, there is a common structural pattern to be seen in all the saints' sermons from Rheinau, each saint's life demonstrates a particular aspect of holiness and a unique manner through which the cause of the Church is furthered and/or defended. These exemplary lives deserved their places in the original *Rheinauer Predigtsammlung* and warrant their inclusion in this selection of Medieval Swiss-German sermons with translation from Rheinau.

THE TEXT

The script in which the manuscript was written falls within Bernard Bischoff's criteria for "Bastarda," a type of Gothic script he describes as a "book cursive" which evolved and was simplified from the earlier Gothic scripts seen in copies of books and documents.[25] All of the sermons in the Rheinau manuscript, including those in the *De Sanctis* section, are written lowercase, with no punctuation whatsoever. One interesting and potentially fruitful aspect of this Rheinau manuscript is the widespread occurrence of *Strichelung*, a kind of highlighting or shading in another color. The phenomenon described by this German term is seen in instances in which the scribe's pen thickens or fills in certain sections of letters with red ink, most frequently the upper strokes of letters such as b, d, and l, or the s. In several medieval manuscripts *Strichelung* of first letters of words can function as a kind of (added) punctuation. Since there is no punctuation in the Rheinau manuscript and almost all words are lowercase, it might seem logical that these unusual letters represent some form of punctuation. However, closer examination of the texts shows the distribution of such highlighted letters to be almost random. Capitals occur only sporadically, mostly at the beginning of a new sermon or of a new section within a sermon. The German texts exhibit a number of superscripts. Superscript *e* over *o* or *u* indicates Umlaut (over *u* sometimes also diphthong), *o* over *u* diphthong, *v* (= *u*) over *a* and *o* also diphthong-like pronunciation; the circumflex denotes vowel length, but appears in many words (also) as an Umlaut sign, for example in *sûnde* or *ûber*.

---

24. In lines 18-19, "Ouwe, achtent, wie selig der helgen geselschaft ist ..."
25. Bernhard Bischoff, *Latin Palaeography. Antiquity and the Middle Ages* (Cambridge: Cambridge University Press, 1990), 136-42.

The Transcription and the Edition

In the transcription of the pages of the Rheinau manuscript, one page of the transcription does not exactly correspond to one page in the original manuscript, however each line of the transcription is the exact length of that particular line in the original. Page numbers within parentheses in the right-hand margin of the transcribed text indicate the beginning of a new page in the original manuscript. The transcription of the original text in this manner duplicates the page format of the manuscript, shows the ways in which the scribe(s) rendered his texts and undertook breaks at the end of lines,[26] thus giving the reader a general feel for the layout and organization of the texts in this fifteenth-century manuscript.[27] The editor has capitalized the beginnings of sentences as well as all names, and added all marks of punctuation throughout. The punctuation closely follows the modern German system as codified by Konrad Duden in the nineteenth century.

In our manuscript the letter *v* is often used instead of *u* in vocalic function, especially at the beginning of words, as in *vnd* or *vf;* for the sake of clarity I have rendered this *v* as the vowel *u*.

For technical reasons the editor has simplified the superscript system in the manuscript somewhat by rendering the superscript *e* as Umlaut and by lowering the superscripts *o* and *v* (= *u*) to in-line vowels, e.g., *frölich, guot, ouch.*

Underlined letters in the transcription indicate resolutions of marks of contraction or suspension. For example, the form it<u>em</u> means that the original manuscript has only *it* with a suspension sign over the *t*. This practice can also be seen in the interior of a word, as in the case of betrachte<u>nt</u>, with a contraction stroke over the second *e* in the original text.

Although the German text has been written quite carefully, some emendations and conjectures are necessary. Letters and, occasionally, entire words in square brackets indicate erroneous or confusing entries by the scribe, as in *min[n]en* ("my", not "love"), which should have been written in the manuscript as *minen*. Occasional dittographies and repeated phrases have also been enclosed in square brackets; the reader thus can easily see where the scribe's eye jumped back.[28] Letters and

---

26. A strong case, incidentally, could be made that it was one hand, which wrote the entire *De Sanctis* section of the *Rheinauer Predigtsammlung*.

27. The line numbers in the left margin of each transcribed sermon are repeated in the English translation so as to help the reader find the original text, if needed.

28. Such cases make clear that the exemplar that the scribe copied was written, not heard.

sometimes whole words in pointed brackets indicate letters or words left out of the text, which should have been included for a correct or minimal understanding, as we see in the clause *und sant Anderes \<es\> ersach*. If a correction couldn't be done by these simple means of bracketing, the editor uses an asterisk in front of the emended word in the text, giving the manuscript form in a footnote.

In vernacular medieval texts prefixes to verbs are frequently written detached from the verbs to which they belong and which they modify. There are two types of such prefixes in German: Those which are always inseparable, e.g., *be-, er-, ver-* or *zer-* (these are very old) or younger ones (derived from prepositions) such as *um-, über-*; in these cases the stem of the verb is stressed, not the prefix, e.g., *betrachten* "to consider" or *übersetzen* "to translate"; these I have re-attached to the verb in case the scribe didn't. For example, even though the scribe writes *ver stan* in the original, it appears as *verstan* in the transcribed text. Younger prefixes can also be separable, in which case they are stressed (as in English): *ich volge nach* "I follow, imitate" or *ich setze über* "I carry over." The scribe either joins or separates these prefixes. Since modern German isn't altogether logical (because it joins the parts in certain cases such as the infinitive or the past participle), I have decided not to regulate these verbs, but to render them as they appear in the manuscript, so that one finds the forms *nach volgen* as well as *nachvolgen* (modern German only: *nachvolgen*). The scribe also quite often separates or joins words or word elements that shouldn't be, as for example in compounds such as *kouf man,* "merchant," on the one hand; *spracher,* "he spoke," on the other. In such cases the editor re-attaches or divides in an intelligent way, usually following the rules of modern German. In all cases of doubt or possible linguistic flux he gives the readings of the manuscript, so that the transcription shows one of both forms, e.g., *davon* or *da von* "thereof, therefore."

THE TRANSLATION

In view of the intended scholarly readership of the "Reformation Texts With Translation," the translator saw it as his task to translate the texts as accurately as possible into modern American English. The translation, therefore, is as literal as possible, becoming somewhat freer if needed. Thus the original rhythm of this prose with its markedly oral character has been preserved to a great extent. Unfortunately, the so strongly Latinized English language cannot do justice to this Swiss dialect which uses almost exclusively German vocabulary, not foreign or loan words. It would have been nice if one could have captured the flavor of this late-medieval Swiss-German dialect, but one would have had to recur to, let us say, Chaucerian English to do so adequately. The reader may be encouraged to simply read, on occasion, a page or so of the original aloud.

In the following pages, the reader is offered a compendium of the salient points of each saint's sermon in this edition.

Sermon Summaries:

What to look for...

The Sermon on Saint Andrew

The biographical information at the beginning of the sermon shows St. Andrew as a believer demonstrating an extraordinary desire to live out his life as an imitation of Christ, to the point of undergoing his own passion and death. The preacher lays particular emphasis in l. 6 on Andrew's willingness to suffer hardship for Christ's sake. St. Andrew is seen as a courageous figure, longing for, rather than fearing the cross upon which he is to be martyred (ll. 23-30), saying in ll. 29-30 that he has long desired (*lang begert*) to embrace the cross. We see St. Andrew's commitment to the Christian message as he preaches to the assembled crowd of onlookers after he has already been hung on the cross (ll. 55-56). The preacher cites two benefits St. Andrew derived from his martyrdom (ll. 30-40): (1) that he had God's love in his heart[29] and (2) that St. Andrew experienced a perfection of virtue. The preacher goes on to say there is a benefit to be reaped by the believer who venerates St. Andrew: that the more someone trusts St. Andrew, the stronger the believer becomes in his martyrdom and in respect to virtues.

In the exemplum comprising the second half of the sermon (ll. 82-163), St. Andrew demonstrates that he will assist anyone who honors him and calls upon him. In this exemplum St. Andrew saves a bishop and overcomes the devil in an engaging tale which offers a great deal of entertainment value. In the exemplum, it is one no less than a bishop, here a bishop who held St. Andrew in great esteem, who is tempted by the devil. There are disguised identities here, which are revealed by the end of the tale: The devil appears in the

---

29. It is this love which enables St. Andrew to follow God up to the point of death on the cross (ll. 31-39).

form of an attractive, seductive young lady, apparently an allusion to Eve, through whom man fell. St. Andrew, disguised as a wandering pilgrim, rescues the bishop by answering three questions posed by the devil in the guise of the temptress. The dramatic tension increases as the devil (the attractive young woman) asks the pilgrim (St. Andrew) two questions of a general nature.[30] St. Andrew's witty answer to the third question, "How far is it from heaven to hell?" reveals the true identity of the young lady and thereby saves the bishop from further temptation, who finally recognizes the fortuitous intervention of his favorite saint.[31]

The Sermon on Saint Nicholas

The sermon begins with the preacher treating the theme of transitoriness in ll. 2-22. In the description of Nicholas' infancy, we witness in ll. 32-36 a prophetic action, i.e., the baby standing upright on his own while being bathed is a presaging of his "standing in eternal life." Nicholas, chosen as bishop by the people, rather than being appointed by the pope in Rome, was the type of church administrator for whom the church community had prayed to God in ll. 62-71. The saint is also seen in the role of a rescuer saint of endangered seafarers in ll. 74-83, a scene modeled on the account of Christ stilling the sea in the Gospel of St. Matthew 8:26. We can see the basis of St. Nicholas' role in Western European Christmas traditions in the legend of his assistance to the man and his daughters in ll. 47-62. In the exemplum told in the sermon, Nicholas works for financial justice as he aids a Jew who is swindled out of his money by a dishonest Christian in ll. 83-145.[32] The conversion of the Jew at the end of the tale also leads to a new life for the dishonest Christian merchant.

The Sermon on St. Thomas

In this sermon we see St. Thomas overcoming his doubts through obedience to Christ, Thomas ultimately becoming a quite positive figure. In ll. 92-105 of the sermon, Thomas diverts funds intended for the king's construction project to aid the poor. Christ arranges for

30. The questions are (1) "What's the greatest miracle God ever wrought in a small place?" and (2) "Where in the world is it the highest place?"

31. The answer almost has the effect of a "punch line."

32. Here we have a reversal of expected practices in relation to money. Throughout the Middle Ages, Jews were depicted as dishonest money-grubbers. In this case, it is a Christian who cheats a Jew out of his money.

Thomas to be sent to India to undertake his missionary work.[33] We should note in ll. 83-91 the miraculous journey which Thomas and the king of India's representative experience, i.e., making the passage to India in three months rather than three years. Then the king's brother, who dies and then returns from the dead, tells the king about the palace St. Thomas had built for him in heaven. Thus we see a concrete representation of Christ's admonition to gather treasures in heaven rather than on earth (Luke 12:33). Thomas meets his end when a heathen priest in India kills him with a spear in ll. 111-17. As such, this is a typological/postfigural treatment of Thomas' death, harking back to the piercing of Christ's side at the end of his crucifixion.

The Sermon on St. Stephen

The preacher introduces the relationship of St. Stephen and St. Paul to each other, speaking of how the Lord used the sheep to capture the wolf in ll. 6-9. St. Stephen is described as being as mild as a sheep (ll. 9-10) and St. Paul as troublesome as a wolf (ll. 10-4).[34] And despite the fact that Stephen and Paul were at odds with each other during their earthly lifetimes, they now, in ll. 18-23, enjoy the blessed communion of saints in heaven. The preacher sets St. Stephen's intellectual abilities on par with those of St. Paul, with whom Stephen is said to have attended school in Jerusalem (ll. 27-30). We see in the sermon a representation of Christ as a healer (ll. 31-6). In ll. 54-58, the tradition of Veronica and the cloth bearing Christ's image also finds its way into the sermon text. St. Stephen, whom the text recognizes as the first martyr after Christ in ll. 112-15, displays extraordinary wisdom and courage in the face of his Jewish accusers and executioners, who originally sought to have him undertake a legal defense of the Jewish community of Jerusalem before a wrathful Roman emperor.[35]

The Sermon on Candlemas

The preacher tells the congregation in ll. 2-40 of the link between today's feast day and the rite of purification Moses established for

33. India, according to medieval geography, was at the end of the world. In sending Thomas far to the East, Christ goes against the grain insofar as the development and spread of culture in medieval culture proceeded westwards across Europe.

34. The image of Paul as a wolf corresponds well to the life of Saul persecuting members of the early church, and Paul himself, converted, and a strong advocate for Christ, could easily be seen "as mild as a sheep."

35. The infirm Caesar Tiberius is angry with the Jews of Jerusalem who killed this healer on whom the emperor wanted to call.

women after giving birth to children, as well as noting in ll. 52-56 St. Mary's visitation of St. Elizabeth prior to Christ's birth. Throughout the sermon there is a progression from the theme of great sorrow, as seen in the prophecy of St. Mary's grief at Christ's crucifixion (ll. 16-24), which eventually leads up to the image of candles and great joy. In ll. 41ff. there is a highly rhetorical hymn of joy in which St. Mary, in giving birth to the world's savior, gave birth as a benefit for all women: maidens, wives, and widows. There are also two tales in this sermon in which St. Mary figures prominently: (1) A Beguine (lay sister)—at home and unable to attend a church service—is swept up in what appears at first to be the hallucination of a candlelight service, but the evidence of the candle fragment after the vision and the miracle associated with it speaks to the contrary in ll. 80-126. (2) Also covered in ll.126-60, there is the tale of the Jewish boy whom St. Mary saves from a burning fire. Jacobus da Voragine includes this second tale in the information his *Legenda Aurea* offers on the assumption of St. Mary.[36]

THE SERMON ON ST. BENEDICT

From l. 3 on, St. Benedict's spiritual purity and strength is represented by the image of a lily, a completely white flower. St. Benedict is described in ll. 12-14 as being "as white as snow in respect to virtues and purity, especially in respect to living a chaste life." A struggle with sexual temptation is seen twice in this sermon. The devil, in the form of a little bird in ll.15-17, comes to Benedict, and tempts him in a manner such that St. Benedict is only able to overcome this temptation by means of the mortification of his own flesh, described in ll. 19-21.[37] Later in the sermon, there is a more explicit example of sexual temptation, as a cleric jealous of St. Benedict's success, who might be interpreted here as a negative alter ego of the saint, attempts to cause St. Benedict's monks to forsake their vows of chastity by employing seven loose women to dance nude in front of Benedict's monastery. The figure of a bird, here a raven as a counterweight to the tempting bird of ll. 15-17, helps St. Benedict safely dispose of a poisoned loaf of bread which the jealous cleric had sent to Benedict.

There are two miracles attributed to the influence of St. Benedict: After Benedict had given all of the food in the monastery to people suffering from a drought, a huge quantity of flour, enough to replenish the monks' supplies, appears mysteriously before the gates of the

36. Cf. Ryan's translation, vol. 2, p. 87-88.
37. The preacher does not describe the exact nature of this temptation of the flesh.

monastery in ll. 44-56. At one point in the sermon, the devil harasses Benedict's monks who are constructing a wall for their monastery in ll. 37-44. The devil finally knocks the wall down on one of the monks, killing him. But when the monks bring him to St. Benedict, the actions of the saint in ll. 38-41 mirror the account of Christ's reviving Lazarus (the Gospel of St. John 11:43), as Benedict brings the monk back to life.

The Sermon on the Annunciation

It is of significance that the preacher prays to St. Mary at the beginning of the sermon in ll. 3-5 that she may give him the ability to speak of her praise, that she may be praised and we may be bettered as to body and soul. Providing here examples of medieval typological thought, the preacher outlines the chronological correspondences between the Annunciation and other biblical events (ll. 61-118). A biblical citation is read, the Gospel of St. Luke 1:39-51, on St. Mary's visitation of Elizabeth, which event is usually a feast day in and of itself. According to the preacher, St. Mary remained with Elizabeth until John the Baptist was born, which is not the case as the Visitation is described in the Gospel of St. Luke 1:56. The preacher puts strong emphasis on St. Mary's song, the Magnificat, with particular attention being paid to God's elevation of his servant.[38] The concept of God deposing the mighty and raising up the lowly is the theme of the exemplum, ll. 118-224 in the sermon, a very entertaining tale of the king in the bath, the moral of which is the importance of the recognition of personal humility.

The Sermon on Saint Mark

The sermon begins with two quotes from the Gospel of St. Mark dealing with the repayment of believers who have left everything behind in order to follow Christ (the Gospel of St. Mark 10:29 and 30). The preacher presents the dialectic of riches vs. poverty and earthly travails in ll. 13-44. Describing the manner in which great wealth distracts believers from their commitment to the Way, in ll. 13-16, Christ's illustration of the camel being unable to slip through the eye of a needle from the Gospel of St. Mark 10:25 is cited. The preacher

---

38. The fact that the "Magnificat" is said in line 128 to be read/sung during the vespers is of interest. The fact that this is one of the monastic hours might point to the preacher being a Benedictine monk.

also invokes here the interesting image of material wealth as a thorn in ll. 32-34. The preacher brings in another scriptural concept by citing Christ's words from the Gospel of St. Matthew 6:21 on treasures and the heart in l. 40. The preacher ends this section on the dialectic of great wealth and poverty by bringing to the congregation's mind Christ's disregard of material wealth during his earthly lifetime. In an imitation of Christ's life, St. Mark himself lives out the ideal of someone who leaves behind all things of which his previous life consisted in order to serve the Lord.

Whereas it might be expected for a sermon celebrating the life of St. Mark to focus on his authorship of the Gospel, the emphasis of the Rheinau sermon on St. Mark is exclusively on his missionary activity, making the claim that St. Mark was the first to preach to polytheistic heathens in ll. 56-57. The bulk of the information offered on St. Mark concerns his trip to Egypt, eventually to Alexandria, where, according to tradition, he was bishop for a period of time. On the road to Alexandria, St. Mark miraculously heals a cobbler who is accidentally injured while fixing St. Mark's shoe in ll. 67-82, in a manner which parallels Christ's healing of the blind man in St. John's Gospel 9:6.[39]

St. Mark's life is so great an imitation of the life of Christ that there are prominent points of correspondence between Christ's passion and Mark's death. Reminiscent of Christ in the Garden of Gethsemane, St. Mark is at prayer when his enemies seize him in ll. 109-11.[40] As he undergoes his torture, St. Mark thanks and praises Christ for the opportunity to suffer for his sake in ll. 112-17. As St. Mark dies during the second day of his torture, he commends his soul to God in ll. 125-26, as Christ himself did as he died on the cross.

A prominent theme in St. Mark's sermon is that of sudden or unexpected death. The preacher suggests prayer and processions with crosses as a means to ward off unforeseen death in ll. 130-32. The preacher also relates a tale of a series of unexpected devastating crises with which the inhabitants of Rome were once inflicted: drought, famine, flood, wild animals, and even a poisoning dragon in the flood. The preacher of the sermon indicates that this feast day is a day of prayer established by Pope Gregory for the cessation of the devastating effects of this flood in Rome, during which many people died, including Gregory's predecessor, Pope Pelagius (see ll. 156-76). Continuing

39. As the strap on his shoe is broken/torn and when the cobbler injures his hand, St. Mark demonstrates exceedingly strong faith in God that these obstacles will not deter him from his mission to Egypt.
40. These enemies consist of, as it says in line 118, "Jews and other nonbelievers."

the topic of prayer, the preacher cites biblical verses concerning Elijah and the manner in which his prayer led God to effect rainfall in ll. 191-98. The preacher then presents an exemplum on the power of earnest prayer. In this instance, we see the power of a mere mortal to hold at bay a demon acting as a messenger for the emperor of Rome (see ll. 199-236). The sermon ends with an appeal to St. Mark to be our advocate before God in ll. 235-38.

The Sermon on Saints Peter and Paul

Both saints are martyrs who show courage and wisdom in their witness to Christ's message in the face of heathen opposition, first in the person of a sorcerer named Simon in ll.100-186, and ultimately, the emperor Nero in ll. 101-211. The preacher emphasizes the Power of Keys God granted to St. Peter in ll. 6-25 and which is eventually granted to Catholic priests in ll. 16-17, on which the sacrament of confession is based. The preacher speaks of St. Peter's fall into sin through his denial of Christ three times in ll. 89-99, which is described originally in the Gospel of St. Matthew 26:59-73. The preacher explains that God let St. Peter fall into this sin of denying Christ so that Peter might be able all the more strongly to identify with the sinner (see ll. 86-89). It is possible to see the tower scene related in ll. 154-92, where Sts. Peter and Paul oppose Simon the sorcerer and, eventually, Nero, as a narrative tool to have both saints in the same scene, which synchronizes both saints' deaths in ll. 200-207, as well.

The Sermon on St. Mary Magdalene

The preacher tells us in ll. 3-24 of how God illuminated all human hearts with two lights, the sun and the moon. The sun, which illuminates those who are without sin, represents St. Mary, Mother of God. The lesser light, with which more darkness is associated, represents St. Mary Magdalene.

St. Mary Magdalene is a living example of all people who, prior to accepting Christ, have led a sinful life, Mary Magdalene to the extent of demonic possession (see ll. 42-49). The preacher cites Christ's parable of the moneylender and his debtors, taken from the Gospel of St. Luke 7:41-50. It is thus easy to identify Mary Magdalene as an example of the happier of the two debtors who had owed the greater debt. Important aspects of St. Mary Magdalene's earthly lifetime are presented: the fact that she was the first person to whom the resurrected Christ showed himself in ll. 105-7; that she stood courageously at the scene of the crucifixion, unafraid of Christ's executioners in ll. 101-3; and her unbridled love for Christ, which is seen in her washing of Christ's feet in ll. 57-63. A salient point in this sermon is the manner in which Mary Magdalene's life illustrates the dynamic of sin and repentance (see ll. 132-37).

THE SERMON ON THE ASSUMPTION OF THE BLESSED VIRGIN ST. MARY

The preacher of the sermon emphasizes St. Mary's unique entry into heaven with body and soul prior to the Last Judgment in ll. 17-32 . The preacher lists in ll. 40-48 three reasons why we should venerate saints in general, and in particular, St. Mary. The preacher holds up the Blessed Virgin as an outstanding example for all people, especially women.[41] Modern female readers of the sermon might take exception with the reasons from ll. 52-106 which the preacher lists for St. Mary's superior status. Among the reasons presented for St. Mary's exemplary qualities is the fact that St. Mary, in contrast to many women, was not a "chatterbox."[42] Young people in general are also seen critically in ll. 103-14, particularly those young people who gamble away not only their finances but also their lives.[43] In ll. 114-18, the preacher also takes the opportunity to warn the congregation about the three enemies of man: the devil, the world, and the flesh.[44] We should not fail to note the preacher's enthusiasm for St. Mary's effectiveness as an intercessor, including St. Bernard's opinion in ll. 137-55 that St. Mary is the best intercessor. The exemplum of the sermon is the tale of Theophilius recounted in lines 166-238,[45] whose complete spiritual rehabilitation St. Mary brings about following his precipitous fall into sin, as seen in ll. 118-23.

THE SERMON ON ALL SAINTS' DAY

The sermon begins with the reading of the Gospel text of the beatitudes from Christ's Sermon on the Mount (the Gospel of St. Mat-

41. She is more specifically described in l. 55 of the original text as a mirror.
42. She is described in l. 85 as being "nit vilredig."
43. St. Mary, it is said in ll.103-4, never went to any gaming house.
44. See Siegfried Wenzel's comprehensive analysis of this commonplace in medieval literature in "The Three Enemies of Man," *Medieval Studies* 29 (1967).
45. In Jacobus' *Legenda Aurea*, the tale of Theophil(i)us is included in the information he offers on the birth of the blessed virgin St. Mary; see Ryan's translation, vol. 2, p. 157.

thew 5:3-10) with the preacher's extended explication of the text in ll. 4-109. The preacher also offers an analysis of the sources and benefits of earthly financial poverty in ll. 27-33. In his further commentary on the Gospel text, the preacher includes an admonition against swearing in ll. 22-28, and a description of the nature of true mercy (seen in ll. 52-61). The preacher tells the congregation the history of the All Saints' feast in ll. 105-21, and in concluding the sermon, focuses the listeners' attention on the benefits to be reaped from observing the feast in ll. 121-25.

The Sermon on All Souls' Day

The sermon begins with a reference to the Epistle lesson read during the All Souls' Mass, which the preacher says is to be found in St. John's Book of Revelation. The ultimate goal of the feast's celebration is that all souls in purgatory may be comforted (see ll. 10-12). The preacher describes in ll. 16-52 three types of death to which mankind is prone, and the types of prayers to be made for the dead, according to the length of time which has elapsed after the person's physical death (see lines 65-74). The preacher ends the sermon in lines 76-81 with an appeal to make the common prayer for all souls.

The Sermon on St. Catherine

The preacher begins the sermon citing a passage from the Song of Songs and explains in lines 6-10 the correspondences among the images in this scriptural text to St. Catherine. The saint's early life is presented with the events of her life leading ultimately to her conflict with the heathen ruler in Alexandria, as seen in ll. 38-174. In l. 10, we are told that St. Catherine's deceased father was a king named Costus. Having been born into nobility herself, Catherine chooses to follow the true king, Christ, rather than submitting to the false king, the ruler in Alexandria. Catherine considers herself, in ll. 96-100, a bride of Christ.

After St. Catherine comes into conflict with the emperor Matzentius,[46] there is increasing dramatic tension throughout the sermon between the two. Catherine is a living example of the values of truth

---

46.This conflict with the emperr accounts for the majority of the "action" in the sermon, ll. 26-165.

and beauty, whereas the emperor symbolizes the diametric opposite of what Catherine demonstrates through her life.[47]

St. Catherine, as she is presented in this Rheinau sermon, is indeed an embodiment of Aristotle's closely related concepts of truth and beauty. The saint's extraordinary intellectual acumen is in evidence as she defeats the panel of scholars the emperor brings to Alexandria to debate her in ll. 54-74. Despite the physical danger in which she finds herself throughout the sermon, Catherine relentlessly continues to win souls for Christ, converting the assembled scholars during and after the debate of ll. 81-84, and while she is imprisoned, converting the empress and the emperor's top knight in ll. 110-15.

There are some significant miracles associated with St. Catherine in the sermon: (1) We are told in ll. 120-22, after the emperor had Catherine brutally flogged and imprisoned without food and drink, that the saint not only survives, but also is more beautiful than ever. (2) When the emperor attempts in ll.136-40 to martyr her with the wheel of knives, this apparatus of execution self-destructs. And (3) in ll. 174-81, healing miracles in conjunction with St. Catherine's relics are cited. The preacher concludes the sermon in ll. 181-89 by explaining why we pray to St. Catherine.

---

47. He is easily the cruelest character imaginable, not only in his treatment of St. Catherine, but also in the manner in which he executes, in ll. 143-151, his own wife for having converted to Christianity.

TEXTS

Dis sint die bredigen von den helgen und   (p. 297)
des ersten von sant Anderes, it<u>em</u>:

Wir sint hût begand des grossen herren sant
Anderes dag, als er die martter durch got wolt
5   liden und ouch durch gottes willen leit an dem
crûtz, dar an er ouch sin end nam und von diser
bössen welt schied. Und dise wort, die ich in letin
vor gesprochen han, die mocht sant Anderes wol
sprechen, wan si sprechent in dûsch, "ich wil uff
10   den balmboum klimen und wil begriffen sin
frucht," recht als er spreche, "ich wil die marter
liden an dem crûtz, das da gebildet ist nach
gottes krûtz, das glichet dem *balmboum."[1]
Uff disem balmboum gewan und begreif der
15   guot sant Anderes dise frucht, die erst was ein
bewerung und ein zeichen gottes minn. Da
von spricht sant Petterus, "Gott, der haut die martter durch ûns geliden ûns zuo einer bischaft,
das wir im nach volgen." Diser bischaft volget
20   nach der guott herr sant Anderes, wan do in
Egeas wolt martteren, und do man das crû-
tz bracht, und sant Anderes <es> ersach, do sprach (p. 298)
er, "O, seliges krûtz, wie han ich dich so la<u>ng</u> begert ze sechen! Bis wilkomen, guottes krûtz!
25   Gott hett dich mit sinem lip gewicht und gehelget. Davon lid ich an dir gern die marter
und ich kum frölich zuo dir und mit sicherm
hertzen, das du ouch mich frölich empfachest, das
iunger an dir hieng <u>Jesus</u> Chri<u>stus</u>, wan ich han la<u>ng</u>
30   begert, das ich dich vmb vieng." Also gewan und
enpfieng der guott sant Anders den ersten nutz,

---

1. blamboum

These are the sermons on the saints and the first on Saint Andrew:

We're celebrating today the day of the great lord Saint Andrew, as he wanted to suffer martyrdom for God's sake, and also for God's sake (line 5) suffered on the cross on which he also met his end and left this evil world.[1] And these words which I read before to you in Latin, Saint Andrew might well speak them himself, for they read in German, "I want to climb up onto (10) the palm tree and want to grasp its fruit," just as if he were saying, "I want to suffer martyrdom on the cross, which is formed after Jesus' cross, which resembles the palm tree." On this palm tree (15) good Saint Andrew won and grasped this fruit, which was first of all a verification and a sign of God's love. St. Peter said concerning this, "God suffered martyrdom for our sakes as an example to us, that we should imitate him."

The good man Saint Andrew followed this example (20), for when Aegeas wanted to martyr him, and when they brought on the cross, and Saint Andrew saw it, he then said, "Oh blessed cross, how have I desired for such a long time to see you![2] Welcome, noble cross! (25) God had consecrated and sanctified you with his body. For that reason I gladly suffer martyrdom upon you and I come cheerfully to you and with a certain heart, that you will cheerfully receive me too, you on whom Jesus Christ more recently hung, for I have long desired to embrace you."

(30) Thus good Saint Andrew won and received the first benefit,

1. The cross of St. Andrew is distinct from Christ's. Andrew's being in the shape of the letter x is seen later on the flags of Scotland and the Confederate States of America.

2. In the story on St. Andrew in the Legenda Aurea by Jacobus da Voragine, there is a Roman proconsul in Achaia by the name of Aegeas, whose wife St. Andrew converted as well as many other people in the land, thereby incurring the wrath of the ruler.

das ist, das er gottes minn hatt in sinem hertzen und gott nach volget untz an den dot
des crûtzes; und da von mocht er wol sprechen,
35   "Min fuoss, der ist nach gevolget sinem wege,"
das ist, also gott durch min[n]en willen hette
erliten den dod an dem crûtz, also han ich im
nach gedreten an das crûtz, dar an ich durch
gott wolt liden den dot. Der ander nutz was
40   ein folkomenheit der tugent. Da von lessent
wir, so man im ie me drouwt und dett, so er ie
me starker wart an siner martter und an
dugenden. Wan wir lessent von im, do er gebunden wart an das crûtz, und des rich-   (p.299)
45   ters bruoder und ander lût, die zuo siner marter warent kome<n>, sprachent so, "Man sölt einen
milten man, einen helgen man, nit also marttren,"
do brediget sant Anderes an dem crûtz und man-
net si und sprach, "Die martter, die der mensch hie
50   geliden mag, nit gelichet der ewigen fröt, die
er dar umb enpfachet." Und die lût, wol dusent
menschen und des richters bruoder giengent
zuo des richters hus vnd sprachen, "Man sölte einen
so helgen lerer und meister nit also verderben,
55²   der zwen tag lebendig an dem crûtz hieng
und die lût lerte; man sölt in ab dem crûtz nemen." Do wolt der richter Egeas das volk eren
und gieng mit inen und sprach, er welt in ab
dem crûtz nemen. Do in sant Anderes ersach,
60   do sprach er, "Egeas, was wiltu her, wiltu gloubig werden? So wil dir gott all din sûnd vergeben. Bistu aber darumb herkomen, das du
mich ab dem crûtz nemest, so soltu wissen, das
mich niemen ab disem crûtz mag nemen
65   lebend, wan ich han gott gebetten, das er min

2. derben marked out at the beginning of line, tag marked for insertion after
zwen

that is, that he had God's love in his heart and followed God
up until death on the cross. And concerning this he might
well say, (35) "My foot has followed his path"; that is, "to such
an extent that I would suffer death on the cross for the sake of
God's love. I have thus followed up to the cross."

(40) The second benefit was a perfection of virtues.[3]
Concerning this we read, that the more they threatened him
and treated him accordingly, he became increasingly stronger
through his martyrdom and in his virtues. For we read
concerning him, that when he was bound to the cross and
the ruler's (45) brother and other people who had come to
his torture said, "One shouldn't thus torment such a gracious,
holy man," Saint Andrew preached on the cross to them
and admonished them, saying, "The martyrdom which one
can suffer here, (50) does not equal the eternal joy which he
receives for it." And the people, probably a thousand people,
and the ruler's brother, went to the ruler's house and spoke
thus, "One shouldn't kill such a holy teacher and master
this way, (55) who hung for two days alive on the cross, and
taught the people; he should be taken down from the cross."

Then the ruler Aegeas wanted to honor the people
and went along with them and said that he wanted to take
him down from the cross. When Saint Andrew saw him,
(60) he said, "Aegeas, what do you want here, do you want to
become a believer? Then God will forgive you all your sins.
But if you've come here for the purpose of taking me down
from the cross, then you should know that no one can take
me down from this cross (65) alive, for I have asked God that
he take my

3. That is, meant here is a perfection in the imitation of Christ, one (often the
second) of the official requirements for holiness.

sel nem, e das ich kom ab dissem crûtz." Do
*giengent[3] dar, die in hatten gebunden an   (p. 300)
das crûtz und woltent in enbinden. Do er-
lametten in die hend und mochten in nit an
70 griffen. Do *ruoft[4] sant Anderes mit einer grossen
stim und sprach, "Herr Iesus Cristus, ich bit dich,
das du min sel nemest, e das ich kome von disem
crûtz." Do kam zehand ein grosser schin, also das
man in nit mocht gesechen, und weret der
75 schin ein guote wil. Do der schin zergieng, do
schied sin sel von sinem lip und ward sel
von den englen enpfangen und gefürt zuo
dem almechtigen gott. Nun umb das, das wir
im alle dester williger sigent ze dienen und
80 in ze erent mit allen den guotten werken, so
wir im ze lop und uns zuo heil geduon kûnent,
so wil ich von im sagen ein hûbsch bischaft. Wir
83[5] lessent, das einest was ein bischoff, der was
[was] ein helger man und hatt sant Anderes also
85 liep, das er alles das dett, das man in batt[e]
durch sinen willen, und eret in, so er kond oder
mocht. Dissen helgen bishoff hett der tûfel gern
vervelt in in dötlich sûnde. Und macht sich der
dûfel und ziert sich uff in einer hûpfschen frou-
90 wen bilt und kam zuo disem helgen bischof, do   (p. 301)
er mess hatt gesprochen, und batt in, das er ir bicht hortte. Si wer von veren landen zuo im komen
durch rattes willen und were eins hochen
kûngs dochtter, der hett si gemechelt einem
95 man. Und wer si dem endrunen, wan si behielte
gern iren magtuom. Do sprach der bischoff, das
si beitete untz nach dem imbis, so wölt er ir gern rautten, was er guottes kûnd durch des guoten

---

3. gian gant
4. rouft
5. item written in left-hand margin slightly above line

soul before I come down from this cross."

Then those who had bound him to the cross went
there and tried to unbind him. Their hands then grew lame
and they weren't able (70) to grasp him. Saint Andrew then
called out in a loud voice and said, "Lord Jesus Christ, I ask
you to take my soul before I come down from this cross."

Then at once, a great light came over the site such
that one couldn't see him, and (75) the light lasted a good
while. When the light dissipated, his soul then left his body,
and his soul was received by the angels and led to almighty
God.

Now to the end that we are all the more willing to
serve him and (80) honor him with all the good works we can
do in his praise and to our salvation, I want to tell you a nice
exemplum.[4]

We read there was once a bishop, who was a holy
man, and he held Saint Andrew so (85) dear that he would do
everything which one would ask him to do for St. Andrew's
sake, and honored him however he knew how to or could.

The devil would have gladly made this holy bishop
plunge into deadly sin. And the devil dressed himself up
as an attractive (90) woman and came to this holy bishop,
when he had just conducted mass, and asked him to hear her
confession. She claimed to have come from a distant land for
advice, and to be the daughter of a powerful king, who had
married her to a man. (95) And she had run away from him,
because she would gladly preserve her virginity.

Then the bishop said that if she waited until after his
meal, he then would gladly advise her concerning whatever
good

4. The exemplum might be thought of as an 'object-lesson,' or even a 'case
study.'

sant Anderes willen. Und won si hatt ge-
100   sprochen, das si eins kûngs dochter were, do hiess
er si sitzen an *sinem⁶ tische,und in dem si aussen,
do macht der tûfel dem bischoff so gross anvechtung in sinem hertzen und so bös gedenk, [und] das er
siner sel und siner er vergass und gottes, und si an
105   sach so dik, das er in sinem hertzen verviel und
kam in den willen, so er es erst möcht getuon, das
er denn sûnd mit ir wölte began. Und so er also
sitzet und gedenket, wie er es an gelege, das si im
werd, so kumpt ein bilgerin an das tor, klopfet
110   und hiess sich in laun, er welte zuo dem bischof. Do
sprach die frouwe zuo dem bischof, er sölt in nit
heissen in laun, es wer denn, das er antwirte   (p. 302)
einer frag, die si in wölt fragen, und wie er
das könd gesagen, so sölt man in in laun. Der bi-
115   schoff hatt die red stet, und geviel im wol, und
enbout die frouw dem bilgerin. Und sprach also
zuo dem, der wart, "Gang hin und frag den bilgerin, welles das gröst wunder sig, das got
ie getett an einer kleinen statt?" Do antwirt
120   im der bilgerin, "Das wer das gröst wunder
und zeichen, das so meng mensch geborn ist
uff ertrich und doch enkeins dem andern gelich ist an dem antlit, das doch nun einer spa-
n[g] lang ist." Der bott kam und sait dem bischouf
125   und der frouwen dise red, und geviel dem
bischoff gar wol. Die frouw sprach, "Er muoss
ûns noch me sagen, sit das er also vil kan.
Man sol in fragen, wa das ertrich aller-
höchst si in aller welt." Der bott fragt den
130   bilgerin; der antwirt und sprach also, "Da
gott ob allen englen und helgen sitzet, got
und mensch mit ûnser nattur, da haut er
einen irdeschen lip an sich genomen, da ist

6. sinen

advice he could give for the sake of good Saint Andrew. And since she had (100) said that she was a king's daughter, he had her sit at his table, and as they were eating, the devil brought so much temptation into the bishop's heart and such evil thoughts, that the bishop forgot his and his honor and God, and he looked (105) at her so frequently that he succumbed in his heart, and he came to the intention that—as soon as he could do it—he wanted to commit sin with her.

And as he thus sits and considers how he might arrange it for her to become his, then came a pilgrim along to the gate, knocked and (110) asked to be admitted, as he wanted to see the bishop. Then the woman said to the bishop, he shouldn't let him in unless he answered a question which she wanted to ask him, and according to how he answered it, one should then let him in. The (115) bishop accepted the deal, which pleased him well, and had the woman speak to the pilgrim through a messenger.

And she thus said to him, who was waiting, "Go ask the pilgrim, 'what is the greatest miracle that God ever wrought in a small place?'"

(120) Then the pilgrim answered him, "That would be the greatest miracle and sign, that so many people have been born on earth and yet no one has the same face as any other, which is nevertheless only one span long."[5] The messenger came and said this to the bishop and the woman, which pleased (125) the bishop quite well.

The woman said, "He has to tell us more, since he knows still more. He should be asked 'where the earth is highest in the world?'" The messenger asked the (130) pilgrim, who answered and spoke thusly, "There where God sits above all the angels and the saints, God and man with our nature, where he took on an earthly body, there is

---

5. This is, in effect, the breadth of an outstretched hand.

das ertrich aller höchst." Dise antwirt seit   (p. 303)

135   der bout dem bischoff wider umb. Die frouw
sprach, "Wie vil er nun kan, so *kumt[7] er doch nût
her in, er kûnn ûns denn der dritten frag
geantwirten." Si sprach, "Gang hin und frag
in, wie hoch es si von dem himel untz in die

140   helle, und wie menge mil es sige." Der bout
fragt den bilgerin. Do sprach der bilgerin,
"Gang hin, frag die frouwen, die gegen dim
herren ze tisch sitzet, die *weis[8] es bas denn
ich, wan ich gemass den weg nie. Si hautt in

145   gemessen, wan si ist der tûfel und wart von
dem himel in die holl gestossen." Do dis die frouw erhort, do verschwein si. Do schickt der bischof den botten balt zuo dem dor, do was der
bilgerin enweg. Do das der bischof vernam,

150   do wart er gar leidig und bedacht sich, das
er unrechten muot und willen hett gehep<t> gegen der frouwen. Und kam ze rûwen und bat
gott und den guotten zwölfbotten sant Anderes, das er im kunt dette, was er meinte.

155   Do wart im gekûndet, das die frouw der tûfel   (p. 304)
wer und in gern hette vervalt in dötlich sû-
nd von reinem und helgem leben, und das
der bilgerin was der guott sant Anderes und wolt in warnen und behuot-

160   en. Do der bischoff vernam, *das[9] in sin helge, der guott herr sant Anderes, also hett besch-
irmt und behüt, do dienet er im dannent
hin zwifalt me denn e. Da von wellent
wir die helgen dienen, das wir den guote̲n̲

165   herren sant Anderes <bitten>, das er ûns die sinn
gep, das wir in und ander helgen also

7. kunt
8. wies
9. und

the earth the absolute highest." The messenger repeated this answer (135) to the bishop.

The woman said, "However much he knows, he still can't come in, unless he can answer a third question." She said, "Go and ask him how far it is from heaven (140) down into hell, and how many miles it is?" [6]

The messenger asked the third question. Then the pilgrim said, "Go and ask the woman who's sitting opposite your lord at the table. She knows it better than I, for I never measured the way. She (145) measured it, because she's the devil, and was cast out of heaven into hell." As the woman heard this, she immediately vanished. Then the bishop sent the messenger quickly to the gate, but the pilgrim was gone. When the bishop heard this, (150) he became quite sorrowful, and thought to himself, realizing that he had had wrong intentions and bad wishes toward the woman.

And he came to repentance, and asked God and the good apostle Saint Andrew to reveal to him, what he thought. (155) Then it was made known to him that the woman was the devil and would have gladly caused him to fall away from a pure and holy life by means of deadly sin, and that the pilgrim was good Saint Andrew, and wanted to warn him and protect him in this manner. (160) When the bishop heard that his saint, the good man Saint Andrew, had shielded him and protected him, he then served him from then on twice as much as before.

For this reason we want to serve the saints, that we ask the good lord Saint Andrew, that he give us (165) the inspiration, that we honor him and other saints so much

6. literally 'high'

eren, das si ûnser hütter[10] also sigen an diser
welt, guotte werk an ûns ze bestetgen und
ûns bösse werke uffe ze sprechen, das wir
170   an ener welt von im niemer gescheide<u>n</u> <werden>.

---

10. hutter with superscript v instead of e over u

that they can be our protectors in that they strengthen good works in us and dispel evil works from us, so that we are never (170) separated from him in the hereafter.[7]

---

7. Although a somewhat compact conclusion compared to the conclusion of other sermons, note that this conclusion to the sermon on St. Andrew, the first sermon in the Rheinau collection of saints' sermons, serves to focus the attention of the listener/reader on the importance of not only St. Andrew, but of all of the saints whose feasts are celebrated in the Rheinau collection of sermons.

An sant Nikalaus tag, ein bredige: (p. 304)

Dise wort stant geschriben in dem buoch
der wissagen und sprechent ze tûsch
also, "Des rechten menschen gedenknûst — Prov. 10:7
5   ist ewig, und die mülich red ist im aun (p. 305)
forcht, und alles, das in diser welt zerga-
nkliches beschicht, das wirt alles vergessen."
Und alles, das vor ûns beschechen ist,
das ist alles vergessen, als ob es nie beschen
10   were. War sint die nun komen, die mit[11]
gewalt vor ûns gerichsnet hand, kûng und
keisser, herzogen, frigen, graffen oder ritter?
Wer hett ir guot oder ir er, was lons hant si
empfangen umb das zergenklich leben,
15   das si hattend? Es ist alles zergangen, si sint
tod und ist ir gehûgde gar da hin. Die wûrm
hand das fleisch, das ewig fûr die sel, aber
die gott mit drûwen dieneten an diser
welt, der trost und gehûgd weret iemer
20   und ewenklich, und wirt ir namen niemer vergessen, wan si sint eins worden mit
gott und sint mit im ewenklich geeinbart.
Der selben einer ist gesin der guott herr sant
Nikalaus, von dem man bilich dise wort
25   liset, des tag wir hût begand, wan man
gedenkt sin iemer ewenklichen—die menschen (p. 306)
an diser welt und die engel in ewikeit aun ent—
und wirt die red nit fûrchten, so man spri-
cht an dem iungsten tag, "Gand enweg, ir ver- Luke 13:27-28
30   flüchten in das ewig fûr!" Wir lessent von im
in dem Gulden Buoch, das er bûrtig was von kr-

11. mit ûns, ûns marked out

42

On Saint Nicholas' Day, a sermon:

These words are written in the book of the prophets and thus say in German, "The righteous man's memory (5) is eternal and grumbling speech does not cause him to fear; and all transitory things which happen in this world, all of that, is totally forgotten." And everything which happened before us, that's all forgotten, as if it had never happened. (10) Where now have they come, those who ruled with power before us, king and emperor, dukes, freemen, counts or knights? Who would have their goods and property, what kind of reward did they receive for the transitory life (15) which they had? It's all passed away, they are dead and their memory is long gone.

The worms have the flesh, the eternal fire has the soul, but those who served God with loyalty in this world, their consolation and their memory endures forever (20) and eternally, and their names will never be forgotten, for they have become one with God and are unified with him eternally.

One of these was the good lord Saint Nicholas, about whom one justifiably (25) reads these words, whose day we celebrate today, for one always remembers him eternally— that is, the people in this world and the angels in eternity without end—and they will not fear the words, as it is said at the Last Judgment, "Go forth, you (30) accursed ones, into the eternal fire." We read about him in the *Golden Book*,[8] that he was born of

---

8. This was a Latin resource book on the lives of the saints, Jacobus de Voragine's *Legenda Aurea* .

iechen eins edlen hochen geschlechtes. Und do
der erst geborn ward, do leit man in in ein
schön beki und wolt in weschen. Do stuond er
35　　ein lange wil von im selben ufrecht, das in
niemen huop. Er v<i>eng in zit an staun mit dem
lip, das er in ewigem lebend stünd in ewigen
fröden. Er vieng ouch in zit an stan mit den
tugenden, wan wir lessent, das er in dem
40　　zit, do er *soug,[12] allwuchen zwen tag vastet, die
mitwuchen und den fritag, und in den sel-
ben zwein tagen nit me den einest soug.
Und darnach und er begund wachssen, do fle-
iss er sich göttlich lebens und götlicher kunst
45　　mit grossem fliss und mit ernst. Und do er
wol erwuochs, do starb im vatter und muotter, und ward er si erbend. Und in den selben zitten was ouch ein man in der selben
statt, der was *von[13] grossem richtuom in
50　　gross armuot komen und hatt aber drig sch-　　(p. 307)
ön und wol gewachsen dochteren. Die[s] hiess
er man nemen, das si guot mit schanden und
sûnden gewunnen, und, wie si möchten, das
er und si mit hin kemen, wan gross armuot
55　　nach grossem richtuom gar *bös[14] ze gewonent
ist. Und do das der guot sant Nicalaus vernam,
do nam er sins vetterlichen erbs drig gross
goldknolen und warf die nachtes zuo des armen mans venster in. Und do er das guot
60　　mornendes vant, do ward er gröslich fro[e]
und beriett mit sin dochteren, und also wurdent si sûntlichs lebens überhebt. Aber lessent
wir, das des zittes der bischoff starb in dem
selben bistuom, an dem dem volk gar übel und

12. suog
13. won
14. bes

Greeks of a noble and powerful family. And as soon as he was born, they lay him in a beautiful basin and wanted to wash him. Then he stood upright (35) for a long while by himself, without anyone raising him up. He began early to stand with his body, that he might stand in eternal life in eternal joy. He also began to stand early in respect to virtues, for we read, that he, at the (40) time at which he was a suckling, fasted two days a week, Wednesdays and Fridays, and on the same days nursed no more than once.

And thereafter when he began to grow, he applied himself (45) seriously to a godly life and to godly knowledge. And when he grew up, his father and mother died, and he became their inheritor.

And at the same time, there was also a man in the city who had come from great riches into (50) great poverty, yet had three beautiful and well-grown daughters. These he commanded to take men in order that he would get rich by means of shameful and sinful actions and he and they could get by as best they could, for it is a very unpleasant thing to get accustomed to great poverty (55) after great wealth.

And when good Saint Nicholas heard that, he took three big clumps of gold from his paternal inheritance and during the night threw them in through the poor man's window. And when he found the money (60) in the morning, he became abundantly happy and consulted there with his daughters, and thus they were raised up out of a sinful life.

We read in addition that at that time the bishop died in the same bishopric, where the people (65) suffered much evil and

65   leit beschach. Und do batt das volk ûnsern her-
en gar ernstlich, das er si aber besorgete an
einem so helgen man und innen den *ze erkenent[15] gebe und kunt dete, wer der sin sölt. Do
ward innen kunt gedan, das \<das\> sant Nikalaus
70   sin sölt, und wart er uf geworffen und erwelt zuo einem bischof. Und hielt sich also in
wirdikait, das sin guot lop gar witnes gekûndet   (p. 308)
ward und also wit, das grosse welt zuo zoch umb
das, das si in gesechent. Eins mauls kam ein schiff
75   wol geladen mit lûtten und guot, und viel
aber gar gross ungewitter in mit wind, das
die lût gröslich erschraken. Und do si den guotten
herr sant Nicalaus und nothelfer an ruoften mit
grossem ernst, das er innen ze helf kem. Und ze
80   stund erschein er inen und gestilt das mer und
den wint. Also seittent si im lop und dank, das er
dem wind und dem mer hatt und mocht gebie-
tten. Ouch so lesend wir von einem koufman, der
was vast rich gesin und haut aber das sin gar un-
85   nutzlich verzert vnd vertan, das er nûtz me
hatt. Eins mauls baut er einen iuden, das er im
pfennig lich. Do vordret der iud pfand von
im, als der iuden gewonheit ist, so welt er im
gelt lichen. Der kofman sprach, "Ich han nit pfand,
90   aber ich wil dir ein[n]en burgen gen." Do sprach
der iud, "Wer ist der bûrg?" Er sprach, "Es is sant Nikalaus." Do sprach der iud, "Von dem han ich so vil
trûwens und guottes gehört, ich wil in gern han
zuo einem bûrgen." Also lech der iud dem koufman
95   vil guottes und silbers. Der koufman nam das guot
und warp da mit, das er wol wider umb errichet.   (p. 309)
Und do das der iud verstuond, do iesch er im, das er
im gelichen hatt. Do baut der koufman den iuden ûm

15. zerken/ent

pain. And then the people very earnestly asked our Lord to provide them again with such a holy man and indicate him to them and make known who it was going to be. When it was made known to them that it (70) should be Saint Nicholas, he was proposed and chosen to become a bishop, and he conducted himself with such worthiness, that his good praise was announced far and wide and so far that great masses of people marched to his place in order to see him.

Once a ship came (75) well laden with people and goods, and a great storm came on with such high winds, that the people were greatly frightened. And when they called upon the good lord and rescuer Saint Nicholas with great seriousness, that he might come to their rescue, he appeared to them at (80) once and stilled the sea and the wind. So they gave him praise and thanks that he had been able to command the wind and the sea.[9]

We also read about a merchant who had been quite rich, yet (85) had spent and wasted his wealth so that he had nothing left. Once he requested of a Jew that he loan him some money. Then the Jew demanded a deposit from him, as Jews are accustomed to do, and only then he would lend him money. The merchant said, "I don't have a deposit, (90) but I want to give you a guarantor." Then the Jew said, "Who's the guarantor?" He said, "It's Saint Nicholas." Then the Jew said, "About him I've heard so much that deserves trust and is good; I'll gladly have him as a guarantor." Thus the Jew lent the merchant much (95) wealth and silver. The merchant took the money and managed it in such a good manner that he, in an honest way, once again grew wealthy. And when the Jew noticed that, he demanded that he repay what he had lent him. Then the merchant asked the Jew for another

---

9. Nicholas demonstrates here power over the elements as Christ does in the Gospel of St. Matthew, chapter 8.

einen tag. Den gab er im und det im also zuo drin
100   mallen. Und zuo dem vierden mal, do er im es aber
iesch, do sprach er, er hette in bezalt und sölt im nût
me und lögnet im gentzlich. Der iud manglet sins
geltes unbilich und ungern und bracht die sach
fûr gericht. Also ward dem cristnen erdeilt, das
105   er den iuden ze stund bezalen sölt oder aber mit
uf gehebter hand schweren, das er im bezalt hette.
Also gieng der iud und der koufman zuo sant Nicalaus
kilchen. Nun hatt aber der koufman einen bilgerin-
stab und hatt dar in mit listen golt verwûrkt. Und
110   do si kament zuo der kilchen, do gap der koufman
dem iuden zehant den stap vor der kilchen. Und
gieng der koufman in die kilchen und knûwet
fûr den altar und schwor da, das er dem iuden
hett das guot geben. Do sprach der iud, "Ich getrûw
115   sant Nikalaus wol, er laus das niemer ungeroch-
en." Der koufman nam den stap wider von dem
iuden und ging frölich hein mit sinen frûnden. Und do sin frûnd hein kamen, do wolt er
ouch hein gaun. Und do er uff der straus was, do bestuond
(p.310)
120   in ein so starker schlauf, das er sich nider leit an
dem weg und da entschlief. Und bi einer kleinen
wil, so *kumt[16] ein wol geladner wagen, und do sin
die karerknecht war namen, do schrûwen si
uff in, das er uf stünde. Er kert sich nit dar an,
125   bis das der wagen ûber in gieng und in er-
dott; und sin stap, der bi im lag mit dem golt,
der wart ouch zerbrochen. Und do die karerknecht das golt sachen, do nament si es und gehie-
ltent es uffrecht. Und also wart die sach offen-
130   bar, und dem iuden sin guott wider umb, dar ab
er gar frölich wart und ging snellenklich zuo

16. kunt

day. He gave him that and two more (100) times. When he demanded it again from him, for the fourth time, he said he had paid him and owed him nothing more, and denied the matter to him totally.

The Jew was deprived of his money unjustly and unwillingly, and brought the matter to court. Thus the judgment was made to the Christian that (105) he should immediately pay the Jew or else swear with his hand raised that he had paid him. Thus the Jew and the merchant went to Saint Nicholas' church.

Now, however, the merchant had a pilgrim's staff and had cleverly put gold into it, and (110) when they came to the church, the merchant immediately gave the Jew the staff before the church. And the merchant went into the church, and knelt before the altar and swore there, that he had given the Jew the money. Then the Jew said, "I trust (115) Saint Nicholas for sure that he will never let this go by without revenge."

The merchant took the staff back from the Jew and went merrily home with his friends. And when his friends came home, he also wanted to go to his home. And when he was on the road, (120) such a powerful sleep overcame him that he lay down on the road and fell asleep there. And after a while a well-laden wagon comes along, and when the wagoners became aware of him, they cried out to him to stand up. He didn't pay attention to this (125) until the wagon ran over him and killed him, and the staff lay next to him with the gold, which got broken into pieces. And when the wagoners saw the gold, they took it and held it up.

And thus the affair became (130) manifest, and the Jew's money reverted to him, which made him very happy, and he went quickly to

sant Nikalaus kilchen und lop<t> da gott und sinen
lieben herren sant Nikalausen. Und enthiess ouch
do zemal ûnserm herren und sant Nicalaus, das
135   er sich wölte laussen touffen und sich gentzlich bessren umb das, das der liep herr sant Nicalaus
umb ûnsern herren erwurb, das sin ungetrû-
wer gûlt wider umb zuo dem leben kem. Also
tett ûnser herr ein zeichen durch sinen frûnd[e]
140   und liess in wider lebend werden und kam
ouch dar nach und veriach da[17] siner un-
trûw und missetat. Do aber der iud sach das
gross zeichen, das da geschechen was durch   (p.311)
den guotten herren sant Nicalaus, do liess er sich
145   touffen mit allem sinem husgesind. Bittent wir
den lieben herren sant Nikalaus, das wir ûns
hie in zit also halten, das wir dört von im niemer gescheiden werden. Des helffe ûns gott, amen.

17. da ûwer, ûwer marked out

Saint Nicholas' church and there praised God and his dear
lord Saint Nicholas. And he also then pledged to our Lord
and Saint Nicholas that (135) he wanted to be baptized and
completely better himself, in order that dear Saint Nicholas
might obtain it from our Lord, that his dishonest debtor
would come back to life again.

Thus our Lord did a sign for his friend's sake (140)
and let him, the debtor, come back to life, and he came also
thereafter and confessed his fraud and wrongdoing. But when
the Jew saw the great sign which was wrought for the good
lord Saint Nicholas' sake, he had himself (145) baptized with
all of his household. Let us ask dear Saint Nicholas that we
conduct our lives during our time here on earth in such a way
that we be never separated from him in the life to come. May
God help us with this, amen.

An sant Toman, item: (p. 311)

Dise wort sprach ûnser herr selb zuo sant Domen
und sprechent ze tûsch also, "Thoman, [und sprechent
ze tûsch also, Toman,] wan du mich gesechen hast,
5   da von so gloubestu, aber selig sind die, die mich nit
                                                          John 20:29
gesechen hant und doch geloup\<t\>[18] hand." Von dissen
wortten schribet santus Johanes, der ewengelist,
uff den achtenden tag der helgen urstende, das
uff den selben tag die iunger unsers herren bi
10   enander und gesamnet warent ze Ierusolem
in eim hus und hattent die tûren beschlossen an   John 20:19
dem hus von vorcht wegen der iuden. Do kam
ûnser herr zuo innen und stuond en mitten vn-
der si und sprach zuo inen, "Frit si mit ûch," und
15   nach dissen wortten liess er sich sechen und be-
kenen. Und do si sin minzeichen sachen an henden und an füssen und ouch sin heilgen siten, do   (p. 312)
wurden si gröslich erfrouwet und bekanten
in als iren gewaren gott und menschen. Nun
20   was aber santus Tomas nit bi inen uff das selb
zit. Und do er erst kam, do sprachent si zuo im
mit grossen fröden, "Thoma, wir hant ûnsern
lieben herren gesechen." Do sprach er, "Ich sechen
denn sin hend, die zeichen, da die nagel durch   John 20:25
25   wurden geschlagen, und ich leg denn min
vinger in die wunden siner sitten, so gloup ich
es nit." Dar nach ûber acht tag, da warent aber
die iunger ûnsers herren bi enander—warent
von den zitten sins dodes umb mengerlei
30   hûbscher sachen wegen, der ich durch der kur-

18. partial t after geloup marked out

On Saint Thomas Day, another sermon:

Our Lord Himself spoke these words to Saint Thomas and thus they read as follows in German, "Thomas, because you have seen me, (5) you therefore believe, but those are blessed who haven't seen me and yet have faith." About these words Saint John, the Evangelist, writes that on the eighth day of the Holy Resurrection, on that same day our Lord's disciples were with each (10) other and assembled at Jerusalem in a house and had locked the doors to the house out of fear of the Jews.

Then our Lord came to them and stood amongst them and said to them, "Peace be with you," and (15) after these words, he allowed himself to be seen and recognized. And when they saw the signs of his love on his hands and feet and also his healed side wound, they became greatly joyous and acknowledged him as their true God and man.

Yet (20) Saint Thomas wasn't with them at the same time. And as soon as he came, they said to him with great joy, "Thomas, we've seen our dear Lord." Then he said, "Unless I see his hands, the marks of the places through which the nails (25) were pounded, and unless I put my finger in the wound of his side, I won't believe it."

Eight days afterwards, the disciples of our Lord were again with each other—they were since the time of his death (30) because of many beautiful things which I don't mention for the sake of brevity—

tzerung willen geschwigen—und warent aber
ir tûren vast und ser beschlossen. Do kam aber ûnser herr und stuond en mitten under si und spr-   John 20:26
ach, als Johanes schribet, "Pax vobis, frit mit ûch,"
35   und sprach zuo sant Toman, "Toman, leg din hent
oder din vinger in min sitten und bis nit un-   John 20:27
geloubig!" Santus Tomen was geloubig, gehorsam
und dett, das er *im[19] hiess, und sprach gar balt,
"Du bist min gott und min herr." Do sprach ûn-
40   ser herr zuo im, "Thoman, wan du mich gesechen   (p. 313)
hest, da von so gloubest du. Selig sint die, die mich
                                                              John 20:29
nit gesechen hant und doch[20] geloupt hand." Das
ist das ewangelium. Nun lessen wir fûrbas von
im in der Lambartik—das ist ein buoch, dar inn
45   staut der helig martterer <leben> und verdienen—, das
in ûnser herr dik und vil mante, das er gieng
gen India, das ist ze ende der welt, und da die
lût bekerte. Wan aber das selb volk *alles[21] gar hart
und ungeschlacht was, do wer er gern sust ge-
50   gangen, war ûnser herr in geheissen oder ge-
schickt hette. Und do ûnser herr sinen schrecken und
sin vorcht bekante, do kam er aber eins mauls
und sprach zuo im, "Toman, fûrcht dir nit und
gang in Indian, wan ich wil mit dir sin und
55   wil dich nit laussen und ich wil dinen name̱n
erhöchen. Und solt du min[n]en namen offnen
den lûtten in dem land, und von dem land
wil ich dich nemen in din rich und wil dich
setzen zuo dinen bruodern, wan du solt wissen, das
60   du in dem land muost liden gross arbeit um
minen willen." Do das santus Tomes erhört,
do sprach er, "Ich bitt dich, lieber herr, das du mich,   (p. 314)
dinen knecht, nit da hin sendest, wan das land

19. in
20. doch nit, nit crossed out
21. als

and their doors were again tightly, impenetrably locked. But
then our Lord came and stood amidst them and said, as John
writes, "Pax vobis, Peace be with you," (35) and then said to
Saint Thomas, "Thomas, put your hands or your fingers into
my side and be no longer unbelieving!" Saint Thomas was
believing and obedient, and did what he ordered him to do,
and said immediately, "You are my God and my Lord." Then
(40) our Lord said to him, "Thomas, because you've seen me,
you believe. Blessed are those who have not seen me and yet
have believed." That is the Gospel.

Now we read further about him in the Lambartik—
that is, in the book in which (45) the lives of the holy martyrs
and their merits are written—that our Lord admonished Saint
Thomas frequently and often to go to India, which is at the
end of the world, and convert the people there.[10] But since all
the people there were rough and uncivilized, he would have
rather gone somewhere else, (50) wherever our Lord would
have ordered him or sent him.

And when our Lord recognized his terror and fear, he
came again on another occasion and said to him, "Thomas,
do not fear and go to India, for I will be with you and (55)
will not leave you and I will exalt your name. And you shall
reveal my name to the people in the land, and from the land I
will take you into your kingdom and I will join you with your
brothers, for you should know (60) that you must suffer great
hardship in the land for my sake." When Saint Thomas heard
that, he said, "I beg you, dear Lord, that you not send me,
your servant, there, for the land

---

10. Cf. the subtitle of Th. Grässe's Latin edition of the Golden Legend: Jacobi a Voragine Legenda Aurea: Vulgo Historica Lombardica Dicta. See for this
passage Ryan's translation, vol. I, p. 30; God asks here Thomas only twice.

gar verr ist, und die lût da selbs gar grop und
65   hert sint und bekenet die warheit nit." Doch
so was er gehorsam. Nun was des zittes zuo Ierusolem ein koufman, der was von dem kûng
von Indeian us gesant, das er in allen landen
suochte einen meister, der im machte und buwte
70   einen schönen und costlichen palast. Dissem kofman erschein ûnser herr in eins gerauttnen
manes gestalt und sprach zuo im und fraget
in, was er in disen landen suochte oder schüffe. Do
sprach der koufman, "Mich hett min herr, der
75   kûng von Indegan, gesant in dise land, das ich
suoche einen guotten bumeister, der im einen
palast buwe." Do sprach ûnser herr, "Ich han einen
knecht, der ein meister ist semlichs werks, und
wilt du in, so gang mit mir." Und also fuort
80   in ûnser herr zuo sant Thomen und sprach zuo
im, "Sich, dis ist min knecht, von dem ich dir
geseit han ding, und ûberkum mit im
und für in mit dir." Der koufman tett also
und nam santum Tomen mit im in sin schif   (p. 315)
85   und fuorent in drin maneden untz gen Indegan. Und do der koufman verstuond, das innen
so wol gelungen was und das si so verr kom-
en warent in so kurtzem zit, do erschrak er,
wan vormauls, wenn er den weg in drin
90   iaren gevarn mocht, den er in drin[22]
manotten gevarn hett, so benügt in wol.
Und do er kam zuo dem kûng, do gap er im
gar gross guott, das er im einen palast machte.
Also nam santus Tomes das guot alles und gap
95   es armen lûtten durch gottes willen. Und
dar nach über lang und der kûng des buws
nit sach, do hiess er in vachen und in einen ke-

22. drin iaren, iaren marked out

is far away, and the people themselves there are uncivilized and (65) rough and do not acknowledge the truth." Yet he was obedient.

Now at this time there was a merchant in Jerusalem, who had been sent out from the King of India, that he might seek in all lands a master to build him (70) a beautiful and lavish palace. Our Lord appeared before this merchant in the form of a handsome man and spoke to him and asked him what he was seeking or doing in these lands. Then the merchant said, "My lord, the (75) King of India, sent me to these lands, that I seek a good master builder who might build him a palace." Then our Lord said, "I have a servant, who is a master of all kinds of works, and if you want him, go with me." And thus (80) our Lord lead him to Saint Thomas and said to him, "See, this is my servant, whose capabilities I just mentioned, and come to terms with him and take him with you." The merchant did this and took Saint Thomas with him in his ship (85) and they traveled in three months up to India. And when the merchant noticed that they'd done so well and that they had come so far in such a short time, he was frightened, for previously, whenever he was able to traverse the way in three (90) months which he had traveled in three years, he was quite satisfied.

And when he came to the king, the king gave him a considerable amount of money to build him a palace. Thus Saint Thomas took all the money and gave it (95) to poor people for God's sake. And when thereafter for a long time the king saw nothing of the building, he commanded that he be seized and thrown in a

rker werffen. Und in den zitten, do santus Tomes[23] gevangen lang, do starb
100   des kûngs bruoder. Und von gottes ordnung
ward er wider lebend und lûf und schrei mit
grossem er\<n\>st sinen bruoder an und seit im von
dem herlichen und kostlichen buw und sal, den
im der guotte[s] santes Tomen hett gebuwen
105   in dem himelrich. Do viel der kûng und sin
bruoder und sin land und sin lût dem lieben san-   (p. 316)
tum Tomen ze fuoss und bautten in mit grossem
er\<n\>st, das er si toufte, das er ouch tett. Und dar nach
gieng er durch das land und lert und predi-
110   gett cristnen glouben und leit meng not und
arbeit durch gottes willen. Do er vil erleid,
do wart er ze iun\<g\>st mit eim sper[24] durchstochen
von einem alten ewartten, der da pfleger
was der götten. Also nam er sin end und wa-
115   rt sin sel von den englen gefürt zuo gott in das
himelrich zuo sinen bruodern, den zwölfbotten.[25]

23. mes des buwes, des buwes marked out
24. e of sper superscript
25. again an abrupt ending; cf. the St. Andrew sermon

prison. And at the time Saint Thomas lay incarcerated, (100) the king's brother died. And according to God's disposition he came back to life and ran and cried out to his brother with great seriousness and told him about the magnificent and lavish building and hall which Saint Thomas had built for him (105) in the Kingdom of Heaven.

Then the king and his brother and his land and his people fell down at Saint Thomas' feet and asked him with great seriousness to baptize them, which he also did. And after that he went through the land and taught and preached (110) the Christian faith and suffered great distress and travail for God's sake.

After having suffered much, he was finally run through with a spear by an old priest, who was a keeper of the gods. Thus he came to his end, and his soul was (115) led up by the angels to God into the Kingdom of Heaven to his brothers, the apostles.[11]

11. This is, again, a somewhat abrupt ending; cf. the end of the Saint Andrew sermon.

An sant *Steffens[26] tag, it<u>em</u>:   (p. 316)

Sant Steffen, des tag wir hût begaunt, der ist
hût enbunden von der not diser armen welt.
Und der unmilt mensch, der da was ein durech-
5   ter, sant Palus, der wart an sin statt erwelt
ze lident. Ûnser herr, der durch des sûnders
willen kam uff ertrich, das er den sûnder bekerte, der hett mit dem schauf den wolf ge-
fangen, wan der guot sant Steffen was als
10   senft als ein schauf, aber sant Palus was als
mülich als ein wolf, wan er hatt brief ge-   Acts 9:1-2
nomen von den richtern, wa er ein cristen mensch   (p. 317)
funde, das er den vieng und den brecht den richtern gen Ierusolem. Dire herr sant Palus, der nu<u>n</u>
15   sant Stephan halp versteinen, der wart dar nach
sin bluot vergiessen durch gott und sant Stefen; den
er an dire welt versmachet,[27] mit dem wart er
sitzent in dem himelrich. Ouwe, achtent, wie selig der
helgen geselschaft ist, da enkeiner dem andren vig-
20   ent ist umb das, das er im an dire welt hett ge-
t[t]an. Nun schemet sich sant Paulus nit, das er in half
versteinen. So frouwt sich sant Steffen sant Paulus
geselschaft. Von disen zwein helgen, sant Steffen und
sant Pawlus, lessent wir, das si zesamen giengen
25   ze schuol zuo Ierusolem; und was sant Paulus bûrtig
von der statt Rom, do was aber sant Steffen frömt.
Und warent bed wol gelert, und wurdent dik he-
sslich kriegen von der kunst, wan sant Paulus verstuond die geschrift nach der welt si<u>n</u>, do wolt si
30   sant Steffen nach götlichem sin verstan. Des selben
zittes was ze Rom ein keiser, der hiess Tiberius; der

26. steftens
27. partial letter follows verschmachet

60

On Saint Stephen's Day, another sermon:

Saint Stephen, whose day we are celebrating today, was released today from the suffering of this poor world. And the ungentle man, who was a persecutor, (5) Saint Paul, was chosen to suffer in his place.

Our Lord, who came to earth in order to convert the sinner, had caught the wolf with the sheep, for good Saint Stephen was as (10) gentle as a sheep, but Saint Paul was as troublesome as a wolf, for he had taken orders from the authorities, that wherever he found a Christian, he would seize him and bring him before the authorities in Jerusalem. This man Saint Paul, who now (15) helped stone Saint Stephen, would later shed his blood for the sake of God and Saint Stephen; whom he disparaged in this world, with him he came to sit in the Kingdom of Heaven.

Oh, consider how blessed is the communion of saints, since no one is (20) ill-disposed to the other concerning what he had done to him in this world. Now Saint Paul is no longer ashamed that he helped stone him. On the other hand, Saint Stephen is happy to have the company of Saint Paul.

About these two saints, Saint Stephen and Saint Paul, we read that they went (25) to school together in Jerusalem; and Saint Paul was born in the city of Rome, yet Saint Stephen was foreign. And both were well taught, and they frequently got into debates full of strife concerning the art of interpretation, for Saint Paul understood scriptures according to the sense of the world, whereas (30) Saint Stephen wanted to understand them in a divine sense.

At the same time there was an emperor in Rome named Tiberius.

hatt einen siechtagen lang gehept, und kond in
kein artzet nit generen. Disem wart geseit, das
ze Ierusolem ein artzet wer, der hiess Iesus, der
35   vertrib alle siechtagen aun arbeit, nit wan mit   (p. 318)
wortten. Und sant uber mer, das man in balt
hiesse komen. Der bot kam mit *grossem[28] bruch
ûber mer gen Ierusolem zuo Pilatto, der da
richter und kûng was zuo Ierusolem. Do er im
40   seit, was er wolt, und das dem keiser ze Rom
geseit wer, das er den artzet dem keiser sante,
do sprach Pilattus, er wer tout. Do sprach der bott,
er haut ûbel getan aun des keissers wissen. Do sprach
Pilattus, die iuden wurden an im schuldig, das
45   "die *zwungent[29] mich, das ich in dot." In den dingen
wart [in den dingen wart] dem keisser geseit,
wie er die doten uf hiess[en] staun und andre zeichen vil tete. Do sprach des keisers bott, es wer
nit ein artzet, es wer gott selber, und sprach
50   zuo den iuden, si hettent gott gemartret, und
wie si des nit unschuldig möchten werden, er
welte si all martren. Die iuden erschraken
und bautten in, das er inen einen tag gepe, das
si sich entschul<d>getin. Und in den [den] dingen wart
55   dem botten geseit von einem tuoch, da were an-
gemaulet ein bilt nach Iesus, den die iuden   (p. 319)
marteriten, und von dem bilt geschechen
gross zeichen. Dis bilt erwarb er mit grossen arbeitten und bracht es gen Rom dem kei-
60   ser ze hand. Do der keiser das bilt ersach, do
genas er. Do besant er all Römer und seit in
von dem bilt und gebout den, das si den hetten
fûr einen gott, des bilt so grosse zeichen tette;
und die es nit wolten duon, die hiess er dötten
65   und martren. Aber die iuden, den der tag was

28. grossam
29. zuwgent

He had had an illness for a long time, and no physician knew
how to cure him. He was told that there was a physician in
Jerusalem named Jesus, who effortlessly dispelled (35) all
illnesses without trouble, with nothing but words.

And he sent across the sea that someone have him
come at once. The messenger came with great pomp to
Jerusalem to Pilate, who was ruler and king in Jerusalem.
When he (40) told him what he wanted, and what had been
said to the emperor in Rome, namely that he should send
the physician to the emperor, Pilate said, he was dead. Then
the messenger said, he had done evil without the emperor's
knowledge. Then Pilate said that the Jews were guilty of what
happened to him, that (45) "they compelled me to kill him."

In the meantime, the emperor was told how he
commanded the dead to arise and performed many other
signs. Then the emperor's messenger said, he was not
a physician, he was God Himself, and said (50) to the
Jews, they had martyred God, and if they could not prove
themselves innocent of this, he would martyr all of them.

The Jews were frightened and asked him to give
them one day for them to prove their innocence. And in
the meantime, (55) the emperor's messenger was told of a
cloth on which there was a picture of Jesus, whom the Jews
had martyred, and that because of this picture great signs
occurred.

He acquired this picture with great effort and brought
it to Rome (60) into the hands of the emperor. When the
emperor saw the picture, he was healed.

Then he sent for all the Romans and told them about the
picture and ordered them to consider him a god whose picture
wrought such great signs; and those who didn't want to do it, he
commanded them to be killed and (65) be martyred.

But the Jews, to whom the day had been

geben, die sprachen, es wer unmuglich, das si
gott hetten ertöttet, der lebete und tette wider
ir ler und smachte si. Do hattent si sant Stepfen,
der was noch da nit getouft. Den bautten si, das

70   er in ir wort dette gegen dem keisser und si
entschultgete. Sant Stefen sprach, "Ir sond ûch baus
berautten und sont wis iuden besenden von allen
landen und sont des rauttes fragen, wie ir ant-
wirtten wellent, wan mich bedunkt, das

75   man ûch recht tüge; wan was ûns die wisag-
en von Iesus ie seitten, das hett dire gedan." Dise
ret muogt si gar ûebel und volgetent doch
sines rauttes und besanten die iuden von aller   (p. 320)
der welt. Do das die zwölfbotten [das] vernamen,

80   das sant Steffen den iuden also hatt geantwirt,
do giengent si heimlich zuo im und lertten in den   Acts 6:5-6
glouben und doufften in und hiessen in bredigen.
Do das beschach, do wart er erfûlt der *gnad[30]
des helgen geistes, und dett gott grosse zeichen

85   durch sinen willen. Do kament die iuden zesamen und kriegten mit sant Stepfen, und er   Acts 6:9-10
ûberwand si allsament. Das muot si und viengent in und fuorttent in an das gericht und   Acts 6:12
sprachen, er hett ûbel geredt von Mouses un   Acts 6:13-14

90   hett ir e bescholten. Und do er mocht komen ze
red von ir geschrei, do bewaurt er inen [d]alles,
das die wissagen von gott hatten geschriben,
das das alles was volbracht und bewaurt an
dem, den si hatten gemartret. Do sprach er, "War

95   umb sint ir wider den helgen geist, das ir   Acts 7:51
zwiflent, das er gott wer, wan alles, das er
tett, das ist bewert von den wissagen." Do sach-   Acts 6:15
ent si in an, und was sin red und sin antlit als
eins engels. Und do si hortten, das er seit von

100   Cristo, do grinent si in an und schrûwent si   (p. 321)

30. gand

given, they said it was impossible for them to have killed God, who lived and opposed their teachings and disparaged them.

At that time they had Saint Stephen, who was not yet baptized. They asked him (70) to plead their case before the emperor and have them found innocent. And Saint Stephen said, "You should better confer and send for wise Jews from all countries, and should ask for advice as to how you should answer, for it seems to me that (75) they are doing to you what is right; because what the prophets ever said to us about Jesus, he did." This speech troubled them greatly, yet they followed his advice, and sent for Jews from all over the world.

When the apostles heard (80) that Saint Stephen had answered the Jews in this way, they went secretly to him and taught him the faith, and baptized him, and commanded him to preach. When that happened, he was filled with the grace of the Holy Ghost, and God wrought great signs (85) for his sake.

Then the Jews came together and argued with Saint Stephen, and he defeated all of them. That angered them, and they seized him and brought him to the authorities, and said that he had spoken evil of Moses and (90) had maligned their Law. And when he was able to come to speak above their crying out loud, he proved everything to them which the prophets had written about God, namely that all these things had been fulfilled and proven in him whom they had martyred.

Then he said, (95) "Why are you against the Holy Ghost, that you doubt that he was God, for everything which he did is proven by the prophets?" Then they looked at him, and his speech and his face was like that of an angel. And when they heard him talk about (100) Christ, they wailed and shouted at

uff in und zugent si ir gewant ab und gab-   Acts 7:54
ent das palus ze haben, das si möchten wer-   Acts 7:58
ffen. Und fuortent sant Steffen fûr die statt[e]
und versteinetten in. Und do der guot sant
105   Steffen zerworffen wart, das er nit me
mocht liden, do knûwet er nider uff das   Acts 7:59-60
ertrich und batt gott fûr die, die in verstei-
netten, und sprach, "Sechent her, ich sich die   Acts 7:55-56
himel offen und sich Iesum staund zuo sins va-
110   tters rechten hant. Her Ie[u]sus Cristus, nim   Acts 7:59
min sel und vergip dissen ir sûnd, wan si   Acts 7:60
wissent nit, was si tuont." Diser sant Steffen
spricht, das er der erst were, der gemartret sige, wan er leid die martter ze erst nach
115   gott in dem selben iar und ist sit bi gott gesin. Und do er gestarb, do nament die iuden
sinen lip und wurffent in an da[a]s velt, das
in tier und vogel essen. Do behuot in gott, das   Acts 8:2
er nit berürt wart. Do kam einer, der hiess
120   Gemanuwel, und begruop in erlich. Do kame<n>t
die Römer gen Ierusolem ze rechen gott und
brachent di statt. Und marttretten si etlich
iuden, etlich versanten si ver und verkouften   (p. 322)
si. Und do die Römer ander lût und stett
125   ûberwunden hetten, do die all cristen wurden, do kunt gott, wa sant Stepfens lip begr-
aben was. Und do si in us gruopen, des selben
tags beschachent lxxiii zeichen. Dissen grose_n_
helgen sond ir hût ern mit allen guotten
130   dingen—wan wer den knecht eret, der hett
sinen herren geeret—und rüffent in an, das
er ûch helf, das wir im volgen in dugenden
und duldikeit, das wir allen und fûr si biten,
das wir mit im ouch *loun[31] empfachent. Des helf
135   ûns gott, amen.

31. laun

him and took off their coats and gave them to Saint Paul to keep so that they would be able to throw.[12]

And they led Saint Stephen before the city and stoned him. And when good Saint (105) Stephen was pummeled with stones so that he couldn't suffer any longer, he knelt down on the ground and prayed to God for those who stoned him and said, "Behold, I see the heavens open and see Jesus standing at His (110) Father's right hand. Lord Jesus Christ, take my soul and forgive them their sin, for they do not know what they are doing." This Saint Stephen tells us that he was the first to become a martyr, for he suffered martyrdom as the first one after (115) God in the same year and since then has been with God.

After he had died, the Jews took his body and threw it into the field for animals and birds to eat. Then God protected him so that he was not touched. Then someone came who was named (120) Emanuel, and buried him honorably. Then the Romans came to Jerusalem to avenge God and destroyed the city. And they martyred some Jews, others they sent far away and sold them. And when the Romans had conquered other peoples and cities, (125) when they all became Christians, then God revealed where Saint Stephen's body lay buried. And when they exhumed him, on the same day seventy-three signs occurred.

Today you should honor this great saint with all good things—for whoever honors the servant has honored his lord—and call upon him that he help you, that we follow him in virtues and patience, that we ask for all others and in their name that we with him also receive the reward in heaven. May God help us with this, amen.

12. 'Stones' is obviously the intended direct object of the verb, yet not written in the original text.

An ûnser frouwen tag, der liech<t>mis: (p. 328)

Wir sint hût das hochzit began ûnser fro-
wen und schribet ûns santus Lukas also, "Do das (p. 329)

Luke 2:22-23

zit kam, das die tag volbracht wurden, *die[32] Mou-
5   ses geboutten hett den frouwen ze behalten, und
do man das kint Iesus hin zuo dem tempel braucht,
das man es opferte nach der alten e," und do es
min frouw santa Maria und sin frûnd brachten zuo
dem tem<p>el und es da opfret ouch mit im zwo tu-

Lev. 12:6-8

10   ben nach der alten e gewonheit, do was ein
man, der Simen hiess. Der begegnete ir in dem Luke 2:25
tempel und nam ûnsern herren an sinen arm
und wart wisagent, das das kint wer geborn
zuo einer verdamnung mengen ungeloubigen
15   menschen und zuo einem behalter allen den, die
an in geloupten, und wisag<te> ûnser frouwen, das Luke 2:35
das schwert—das ist gottes martter—wurd gand
durch ir hertz. Gottes martter mocht wol heissen ein schwert, wan also ein vigend wirt über-
20   wunden mit dem schwert, also wart der tûfel
überwunden mit gottes martter. Dise gottes
martter dett miner frouwen sante Marien
also we, als ob ein schwert wer durch ir hertz
gangen. Nun merkent, ist das wir nun hût
25   mit her Simen welent Iesum Cristum an (p. 330)
ûnsern arm enpfan, so sond wir hût mit miner frouw sante Marigen ûnser opfer zuo dem
tem<p>el bringen. In der alten e was gesest, das
die richen frowen nach ir reinung, so si ze
30   kilchen giengen, so solten si ein lamp opfren,

32. das

On our Lady's Day, Candlemas:

We are celebrating today the feast of our lady, and Saint Luke thus writes for us, "When the time came and the days were fulfilled which (5) Moses had commanded the women to keep, and when they brought the infant Jesus to the temple to dedicate him according to the Old Law," and when my lady Saint Mary and his relatives brought him to the temple and sacrificed there also with him two (10) doves according to the custom of the Old Law, a man was there named Simeon.

He encountered her in the temple and took our Lord in his arms[13] and began to prophesy that the child had been born for the damnation of many unbelieving (15) people and as a savior for all those who believed in him, and he prophesied to our Lady that the sword—which is God's suffering—would go through her heart. God's martyrdom may well be called a sword, for as an enemy is (20) defeated with the sword, so was the devil overcome with God's suffering. This suffering of God did so much sorrow to my lady Saint Mary, as if a sword had gone through her heart.

Now note, in case we want to receive Jesus Christ in our arms[14] (25) with lord Simeon, we shall bring today with our lady St. Mary our sacrifice to the temple. It was established in the Old Law that rich women, when, after their purification, they went to (30) church, should offer a lamb,

13. literally 'on his arm'
14. literally 'on our arm'

und die armen frouwen zwo duben oder
zwo durdeltûben. Bi dem lamp merkent
wir ein reines, unschuldiges leben, das wir
an ûns sölten han, bi den tuben ein rûwiges

35   hertz umb ûnser sûnd. Wan wir nit aun sûnde
sint, so mugent wir das lamp opfren, so nement zwo tuben, wan die tub, so si sol singen,
so tuot si, als ob si weine. Also tügen wir den
rûwen an ûnserm hertzen und land ûns

40   leit sin, was wir ie gedatten. So werden wir
hûtt wirdig, die kertzen ze tragen. Bi *den *kertzen[33]
ist bezeichnet, das sich hûtt söllent allerhant
lût fröwen, wan Maria, die rein magt,
hatt allen megten geborn. All witwen sond

45   sich frouwen, wan hûtt enpfieng ein wit-
we gottes sun mit her Simon und opfret
in in dem tempel. Sich söllent hût frouwen
alle, die bi der E mit recht sitzent, wan Elis-   (p. 331)
abet, sant Johanes muotter, die ward hût wi-

50   ssagent und ward erfûllet des helgen geistes gnad. Hût sond sich frouwen die kint, wan
wir lessent, do ûnseri frouw und Elisabet enander gruosten und enander umbfiengent,
do si bet schwanger warent, das sich sant Jo-

55   hanes frout in siner muotter lip, das im got
so nach was. Hût sond sich ouch frouwen alle
lût, wan der alle die welt richtet, den na\<m>
hût her Simon an sinen arm. Da von sol sich
hût frouwen alle die welt, das wir hût ker-

60   tzen tragent in den henden. Dise gewonheit
nam die cristenheit von den heiden, wan in
disem manet heint die heiden ein gewonheit, das si ir abgöten ze eren mit liechtern
die stett umbgau\<n>t, wan si wanden von ir

65   gewalt under sich han gedrukt alle die

33. gott got

and the poor women two doves or two turtle doves.

In the lamb we note a pure, innocent life, which we should have in ourselves, in the doves a penitent (35) heart concerning our sins. Because we are not without sin, even if we can afford to sacrifice the lamb, let us rather take two doves, for the dove, when it is going to sing, it sounds as if it were crying. Thus let us then be contrite in our heart and let us (40) be sorrowful for what we ever did. Thus we will become worthy today to carry the candles.

With the candles it is symbolized that all kinds of people should rejoice today since Mary, the pure virgin, gave birth for all virgins.[15] All widows should (45) rejoice, because today a widow received God's son with the lord Simeon and dedicated him in the temple. Today everyone should rejoice who is rightfully married, for Elizabeth, Saint John's mother, began to (50) prophesy today and was filled with the grace of the Holy Ghost. Today all the children should rejoice, for we read, when our Lady and Elizabeth greeted and embraced each other, when they were both with child, that St. John (55) rejoiced in his mother's womb that God was so near to him.

Today also everybody should rejoice, for He who judges the whole world was taken today in his arms by lord Simeon. Thus everyone should rejoice that we today (60) carry candles in our hands. Christianity took this custom from the heathens, for in this month the heathens have a custom that in honor of their gods they go around the cities with lights, for they believed with their (65) power to have subjugated the whole

---

15. When the context of the dark and gloomy days around February 2 is considered, the radiance of all those candles burning in church is a powerful representation of Christ as the light of the world.

welt. Und wan hût Simon got, der da ist ein
liecht aller der welt, an sinem arm truog
und von im hatt gewisaget, das er were
ein lob und ein liecht aller der welt, da
70   von hett die helig cristenheit geordnet,   (p. 332)
das menglich hût kertzen trüg in siner
hand zuo einer bezeichnung, wan an der
kertzen merken wir gottes menscheit, an
dem liecht sin gottheit. Und da von söllent
75   wir hûtt all kertzen tregen und ze kilchen gan. Der das nit mag getuon, der
sol aber betrachten in sinem hertzen mit
einem guotten willen, wan wir findent
geschriben ein schön mer von disem dag,
80   das wil ich ûch sagen. Es was zuo einem
mal ein frouw, die was ein begin und
mocht nit zuo der kilchen *gan[34] und was
gar beschwert dar umb und lag nachtes und betrachtet das hochzit in îrm
85   hertzen. Und do si also lag in der nacht
mit andaucht, do wart ir geist gezuckt und
gefürt in ein schön mûnster. Da sach si
gott selber staun ob dem alter, und wolt
mess singen. Und sant Laurentzien sach si
90   an geleit als ein ewengeler und sant
Vinzenzien als ein letzner. Und stünde<n>   (p. 333)
da zwen engel, die warent senger und
viengent die mess an und sungen, "Herr,
wir hant enpfangen erbermd enmitten
95   in dem tem<p>el; her gott, nach dinem name<u>n</u>,
so ist din lop über alles ertrich. Din rechte
hant ist vol der erbermd." Do vieng do ûnser herr an und sprach ob dem allter, "Glo-
ria in *excelsis *deo."[35] Do las der guot sant Vinze<u>n</u>-

34. kan
35. exelsdieo

world.

And because Simeon today carried God in his arms,[16] who is a light unto all the world, and prophesied that he is a reason for praise and a light to all the world, therefore (70) holy Christianity had established that everyone should carry a candle in his hand today as a symbol, for in the candle we recognize God's humanity, in the light, his divinity. And for this reason, we shall (75) today all carry candles and go to church. Who cannot do that, he should meditate, though, in his heart with a good intention, for we find written a beautiful tale about this day, (80) which I want to tell you:

There was once a woman who was a lay sister and she could not come to church, and was greatly troubled concerning this, and lay at night and thought about the feast in her (85) heart.

And as she thus lay in the night in meditative prayer, her spirit was caught up and led into a beautiful church. There she saw God Himself standing bent over the altar, wanting to sing mass. And she saw Saint Lawrence (90) dressed as the first lector,[17] and Saint Vincent as the second lector.[18]

And there stood two angels who were singers and began the mass and sang, "Lord, we have received mercy in the middle of (95) the temple; Lord God, like your name, so is your praise across the entire earth. Your right hand is full of mercy."[19]

Then our Lord began and spoke, bent over the altar, "Gloria in excelsis Deo." Then good Saint Vincent

16. literally 'on his arm'
17. reading the Gospel, probably at the lectern to the right from the point of view of the celebrant at the altar
18. reading the second readings, especially the Epistle, probably to the left
19. where God is 'centrally' present

100   zius die epistel und der guot sant Laurent-
zius das ewengelium. Dise frouw was also
in dem geist in ir andacht zegegin. Und do
dis ewengelium gelessent wart, do sant
min frouw santa Maria bi eim engel iegli-
105   chem helgen ein kertzen und sant ouch der
frouwen eini. Si ward gar fro und enpfieng
die kertzen. Und do man solt opfren, do gieng ûnseri frouw und opfret bi dem ersten ir
kertzen und dar nach all helgen. Und do es
110   an die frouwen kam, das si solt gan und opfren, do wolt si nit dar und gedacht, si sölt
dis kertzen behalten. Do hiess man si dar
gan opfren, si wolt es nit tuon. Do gieng ein   (p. 334)
engel dar und wolt ir die kertzen nemen. Die
115   frouw wert sich. Der engel zukt ir si *uss[36] der hant,
was der kertzen was ob der hant, und was[37]
in der hand was und dar under, das behuop
die frouw mit krieg. Und in dem krieg erwachet die guot frouw und kam zuo ir selber und va-
120   nd der kertzen ein stuk in ir hand. Das selb wachs, das si allso hatt behebt, das tett an ir zeichen,
wan es macht si gesunt an irem lip. Das selb
wachs wart schon behaltten und geleit zuo andrem
heiltuom, als billich was. Also dett [das] gott der
125   frouwen die gnad, wan si gern wer gewessen
zuo der kilchen, ob si es möcht han gedan. Es was
eins mals eins iuden kint, das gieng mit andren cristnen lûtten und kinden in ein kilchen.
Und was ob dem alter gemaulet ûnser frou-
130   wen bilt, und hatt ûnsern herren uff der schos.
Und do der priester mess gesang und den
lûtten ûnsern herren gap, do dunkt des iuden kint, wie ûnsers herren fronlichamen, den

36. uff
37. undotted i follows was

(100) read the Epistle and good Saint Lawrence the Gospel. This woman was thus in the spirit in her meditative prayer present there.[20]

And when this Gospel was read, my lady Saint Mary sent a candle to each (105) saint by means of an angel, and also sent the woman one. She became very happy and received the candle. And when the people were to make an offering, our Lady went and made an offering of her candle first of all, and afterwards all the saints.

And when it was (110) the woman's turn to go and offer up, she didn't want to go and thought that she ought to retain her candle. Then she was ordered to go offer, but she didn't want to do it.

Then an angel came forth and wanted to take the candle from her. The (115) woman defended herself. The angel jerked out from her hand what there was of the candle extending above her hand, and the woman held with force that which was in her hand and underneath it.

And in the struggle the good woman awoke and came to herself,[21] and found a (120) piece of the candle in her hand. The same piece of wax, which she had retained in this manner, wrought a sign with her, because it made her body healthy. That same piece of wax was beautifully preserved and placed with other holy relics, as was appropriate. Thus God granted (125) His grace to the woman, for she would have loved to be at church, if she had been able to do so.

There was once a Jewish child who went with Christian people and other children to a church. And above the altar there was a picture of our (130) Lady, and she had our Lord on her lap. And when the priest sang mass and gave our Lord to the people, it then occurred to the Jewish child that our Lord's body which

20. in the church where the service was being held
21. She was apparently no longer experiencing the vision from this point on.

der priester den lûtten gap, wer gelich dem
135   kintlin, das es sach uff dem alter. Do gieng es
hin und enpfieng in ouch, und verwandelt im   (p. 335)
sich in fleisch. Do es das ersach, do lûff es hein
und bracht es sim vatter und seit im, wie im
was beschen. Der vatter wart gar zornig und
140   hiess heitzen ein offen und warf das kint dar
in. Des kindes muotter schrei und weinet, die lût
lûffent zuo und brachent die dûr uff und fundent das kint in dem fûr, und wundert si, das
dem kint nût was beschen. Und do si es fragten,
145   wie es vor dem fûr wer genessen, do sprach
es, "Die frouw, die ich sach in der kilchen uff dem
alter staun, die was bi mir in dem offen und
hatt mich in ir schos und dakt mich mit ir
gewand und liess mir das fûr nit nachen."
150   Do dis die cristen lût erhortten, do schluogent
si ir hend zesamen und loptent gott, der das
kint siner muotter ze lop und ze er hatt be-
schirmt. Do sprachen die lût und fragten des
kindes vatter, ob er sich wölt[38] lan douffen.[39] Do sp-
155   rach er, er wölt sich nit laun touffen. Do namen
si in und wurffent in in den offen und ver-
branden in. Das kint und die muotter und all
die iuden liessent sich touffen, die da warent. Also
beschirmd ûnseri frouw das kint vor dem fûr   (p. 336)
160   in dem offen und ouch vor dem ewigen fûr. Nun
bittent wir min frouw santa Marigen, der tag
wir hût begangen, das si ûns dis hûtig hochzit also gepe ze folbringent, das wir an ener welt von ir niemer werden gescheiden.

38. welt with superscript o above e
39. vertical line follows douffen

the priest gave the people was the same as the (135) little child he saw above the altar in the picture. Then he went up, also received it, and it transformed itself for him into flesh.

When he noticed that, he ran home, brought it to his father, and told him what had happened to him.[22] The father became very angry, ordered an oven to be (140) heated up and threw the child into it. The child's mother shrieked and wept, the people came running to the scene, and broke down the door, and found the child in the fire, and were amazed that nothing had happened to the child.

And when they asked him (145) how he was saved from the fire, he said, "The lady I saw standing above the altar in the church was with me in the oven and had me on her lap and covered me with her robe and didn't let the fire come near to me."

(150) When the Christians heard this, they clapped their hands and praised God, who in praise and in honor of his mother had shielded the child.

Then the people spoke and asked the child's father whether he wanted to allow himself to be baptized. He then (155) said that he didn't want to be baptized. Then they took him and threw him into the oven and burnt him up. The child and the mother and all the Jews who were there let themselves be baptized .

Thus our Lady protected the child from the fire (160) in the oven and also from the eternal fire. Let us now ask our lady also Saint Mary, whose day we celebrate today, that she give us this feast of today also that we may achieve that we never will be separated from her in the hereafter.[23]

22. apparently news of what had happened in the church
23. literally 'in yonder world'

An sant Benedikten tag, item: (p. 336)

Dise wort stand geschriben in dem saltter und
sprechent ze tûsch also, "Der rech<t> mensch wachs-   Hosea 14:6
set an dugen<den> als der gilg und wirt vor gott
5   ewenklich blügend und sinen guotten gesmak
gent." Nun mugent wir wol die wort nem-
en ze lop des helgen herren sant Benediktum,
ûnsers vatters, des tag hût ist, und mugent
in glichen dem gilgen—der gilg, der wis ist
10 in dem bluomen und git ouch guotten gesmaken.
Dise drû ding finden wir an dem guotten herren sant Benediktum: Er was wiss als der
schne und was wiss an allen tugenden und sunderlich an kûschem leben. Wan wir lessent,
15 das der tûfel einest kam zuo im als ein fög-
elin, und die wil er es sach, do kam im in
sin hertz also gross anve<c>htung, das er sich kum   (p. 337)
ûberwand von unkûschi und nach was gegangen
usser der wiesti. Und do er was in der anvechtung,
20 do zoch er das gewand ab und leit sich in torn un<d>
in neslen, untz das im die anvechtung abkam;
und da von hett er an im die wisse des kûschen
lebens. Wir lessent ouch, das er hatt die minn, wan
er was allwegent flisig ze tünd, was sinen bruo-
25 dern an lip und an sel nûtz was. Und da von lessent wir, das er zuo einem maul kam uff einen
berg, der hiess Casinus, und sinen mûnchen half
machen cellen, da si inn werent. Do lag er zuo einem maul an sinem gebett. Do kam der tûfel in
30 einer grûlichen gescheft und schrei mit lutter stim,
er heis nit der gesegnet, er heiss wol der verflücht, und war umb er in also durechti alle zit.

78

On Saint Benedict's Day, a sermon:

These words are written in the Psalter,[24] and thus say in German, "The righteous man grows in virtues as the lily and becomes (5) eternally blossoming before God and giving forth its good fragrance." Now we can well take these words in praise of our holy lord Saint Benedict, our father, whose day it is, and can compare him to the lily—the lily which is white (10) when it blossoms and also gives forth a good fragrance.

We find the following three things in the good lord Saint Benedict: He was as white as snow and was white with respect to all virtues and especially with respect to a chaste life. For we read (15) that the devil once came to him as a little bird, and, while he looked at it, such a great temptation came into his heart that he scarcely overcame the unchaste spirit and almost had given up life in the desert. And when he was in temptation, (20) he took his clothes off and lay down in thorns and nettles until the temptation left him; and for this reason, he bore in himself the whiteness of chaste living.

We also read that he had love, for he was always eager to do whatever was useful for his brothers' (25) body and soul, and about this concern we read that once he came to a mountain called Monte Cassino, and was helping his monks build cells in which they were to stay. At that time he once was praying. Then the devil came in a (30) gruesome form, and shouted with a loud voice that he wasn't called the blessed one, but surely the damned one, and told him why he persecuted him so much all the time.

24. This passage actually is taken from the book of the prophet Hosea 14:6, and it is quoted in the Roman Missal to this day in the mass for Saint Benedict, in the Gradual prayer, after the Epistle: 'Justus germinabit sicut lilium, et florebit in aeternum ante Dominum.' This is the second verse of the prayer. The first verse, which is quite similar, is taken from Ps. 91:13, which might explain the preacher's reference.

Do lag der guott herr sant Benediktum stille an
sinem gebett und wolt dem tûfel nit antwirten.

35   Do sprach der tûfel, "Nun muos ich gan und muoss
dinen mûnchen helffen machen die mur, die
si machent." Und gieng der tûfel enweg, da die mûnch
ein[40] mur machent, und warf si wider nider
uff einen mûnch, das er starb. Man nam den mûnch (p. 338)

40   und bracht in sant Benediktem. Do ward der mûnch uff stand von sant Benedikete gebett, und gebot
sant Benedikt dem tûfel, das er sinen mûnchen
die mur wider muost helffen machen, "Die *mur[41]
muost wider machen!" So lessent wir von im, das

45   zuo einem maul was ein grosse dûri, das vil lûtten von gebresten starb. Do nam der guot santus
Benedikte, was er esiges[42] vand in dem closter,
und gap es den armen lûtten. Dar umb wurdent die andren mûnch gar leidig, wan er liess

50   in dem closter nit wan ein wenig brot. Der guot
sant Benedikte trost si vil gütlich und bat gott,
der niemen nût laut gebresten, der in sinem willen
lebt. Und do zehand wart funden vor des mû-
nsters tor zwei hundert mût wisses mels in

55   seken. Das mel truogent si in und lopten gott,
das er in es hatt gesendet, wan si hattent sin ge-
nug untz zuo dem nûwen. Do der guot sant Benedikt also mit grossem zeichen und mit helgem
leben in der welt schein als ein schön liecht, do

60   begund im ein paff siner gnaden ser hassen,
do er sach, das sin lop so vast wuochs, und hette   (p. 339)
gern sin lop gehebt. Er wolt aber sinem leben
nit nach volgen, und zuo wem er kam, mit dem
rett er ûbel *von[43] sant Benedikte, und wen er

40. tûfel ein, tûfel marked out
41. mur with superscript v above u
42. esiges was, was marked out
43. mit

Then good lord Saint Benedict lay quietly at prayer and didn't want to answer the devil. (35) Then the devil said, "Now I have to go and help your monks make the wall which they're making."

And the devil went away to where the monks were building a wall and knocked it down again on a monk, with the result that he died. They took the monk (40) and brought him to Saint Benedict. Then the monk began to stand up from Saint Benedict's prayer, and Saint Benedict ordered the devil to help his monks build the wall up again, "You have to restore the wall!"

Thus we read about him that (45) once there was a great drought, such that many people died out of need. Then good Saint Benedict took whatever foodstuffs he found in the monastery and gave them to the poor people. Therefore the other monks grew quite malcontented, for he left nothing (50) in the monastery but a little bread. Good Saint Benedict consoled them quite lovingly and prayed to God, who never let anyone be in need who lived according to His will. And immediately there were found before the gate of the church two hundred bushels of white flour in (55) sacks. They carried in the flour and praised God, who had sent it to them, for they had it in abundance until the new harvest.

When good Saint Benedict thus shone with a great sign and with a holy life in the world as a radiant light, a priest (60) began to hate him very much because of his graces, when he saw that his praise grew so much, and would have gladly had his praise. But he didn't want to imitate his life, and to whomever he came, with him he spoke evil of Saint

65   mocht erwenden, das er nit zuo im gieng in
den walt, das dett er. Do er sach, das das alles
nit half und das sin lop allwegent zuo leitt gege<u>n</u>
gott und der welt und das sich vil lût von sinem leben bekertten, do gieng dire paff zuo

70   und nam ein brott und vergift das und sant
es Benedikto und gedacht, das er es esse und
sturbe. Nun floug ein rap alle zit in dem walt zuo
sant Benedikto und nam brot von im. Sant Benedikto nam das vergift brott, das im der paff

75   gesant hatt, mit grossem dank und warf es de<u>m</u>
rapen und hiess in, das er es trüge in die wiesti, das es enkein mensch funde. Der rap nam
das brott und truog es enweg. Und do dar nach
ein wil ward, do kam aber der rap zuo sant Be-

80   nedictus[44] und nam von im sin gewonliche
pfruond und auss do die. Do der unsinig paff sach, das im sin unselt nit mocht geschaden, do
gedacht er, wie er im sine mûnch verboste mit   (p. 340)
unkûsche, und hiess siben bös frouwen nakent ab-

85   ziechen und vor dem closter dantzen, das si mit
inn verviellen mit unkûscheit. Do das santus
Benedikte ersach, do gedacht er, das er sin schuldig wer und sast da einen andren apt und fuor
er dannen. Do stuond der arm paff uff sinem hus

90   und fuogt sich, das er dannen fuor. Do er also stuond,
do viel das hus und schluog den paffen ze dot. Do
das Benedikte vernam, do weinet er, und was im
von hertzen leit. Und der rap floug als vor zuo sant
Benedikte und zougt im den weg uff *einen[45] berg,

95   der hiess Casinus. Da vand er eines abgottes [abtes]
hus. Usser dem macht er ein mûnster und nam
da zuo im bruoder, und dienetten gott. Und al<le>s sin
leben was nit wan vasten und wachen und bette<u>n</u>.

44. nedictus sin, sin marked out
45. einem

Benedict, and whomever he (65) could prevent from going to
him into the forest, he did so.[25]

When the priest saw that all this didn't help and
that Benedict's reputation with God and the world steadily
increased and that many people turned away from their life,
he went about, (70) took a loaf of bread and poisoned it, and
sent it to Saint Benedict, thinking he would eat it and die.
Now a raven flew all the time to Saint Benedict in the forest,
and took bread from him. Saint Benedict took the poisoned
loaf of bread which the priest (75) had sent to him with great
thanks, and threw it to the raven and ordered him to take it
into the desert, in order that nobody might find it. The raven
took the bread and carried it away, and then, after awhile, the
raven came back again to Saint (80) Benedict, and took its
usual nourishment from him and ate it.

When the unwise priest saw that his mischief couldn't
hurt Saint Benedict, he considered how he might lead his
monks astray with unchaste behavior, and ordered seven evil
women (85) to disrobe and dance in front of the monastery,
in order that they might fall into sin with them by means of
unchaste conduct.

When Saint Benedict saw that, he thought that he was
guilty of this having come to pass, and appointed a new abbot
there and departed. At the time the poor priest was standing
in his house, (90) it also happened that Saint Benedict
departed. When he was standing in this way, the house
collapsed, and hit the priest, killing him. When Benedict
heard this, he wept, and he was sorry for him with all his
heart. And the raven flew to Saint Benedict as before and
showed him the way up a mountain (95) which was called Monte
Cassino.[26] There he found an idol's temple. Out of that he made a
church, and took in brothers and they served God.

And his whole life was nothing but fasting and
holding vigils and praying; when fasting, he ate not more than

25. meant are the people who go there to join Saint Benedict
26. This is apparently a recapitulation of what happened above in ll. 23ff.

In der vassten so aus er nit denn einest in der wu-
100   chen un_d las allwegent oder bettet. Do er also gross zeichen und wunders vil hatt gedan, do kunt
er sinen bruodern sinen dott und hiess sich tragen in das mûnster und enpfieng ûnsern here_n,
und nam gott sin helge sel von sinem lip. Und
105   nach sinem tod geschachent vil grosse zeiche_n   (p. 341)
durch sinen willen an siechen und an dûfelsû-
chtigen menschen, die da *besessen[46] warent mit
den bössen geisten. Bittent wir gott von himel,
das er ûns lass geniessen sins helgen lebens,
110   das wir[47] mit sant Benedictus ewe_nklich werde_n lebe_n.

46. bessesen
47. vertical line follows wir

once a week
(100), and continually read or prayed. When he had thus
wrought great signs and many miracles, he announced his
death to his brothers, and had himself carried into the church
and received our Lord, and God took his holy soul from his
body.[27] And (105) after his death, many great signs occurred
for his sake with the infirm and people afflicted with demons,
who were possessed by evil spirits. Let us ask God in heaven,
that he let us savor his holy life, (110) that we will eternally
live with Saint Benedict.

27. Benedict mentions his impending death.

An ûnser frouwen tag, als ir ûnser herr gekû- (p. 341)
ndet wart von dem engel Gaberiel, item:

Bittent min frouw santa Marian, das si mir geb ze
sprechen von ir lop, da von si gelopt werd und wir
5   gebessret an sel und an lip. Dise wort stand geschriben in dem ewengelium, das wir hûtt lessent, und
schript ûns der guot sant Lukas, der ûnser frouwen
sunder kaplan was, und schribt ûns, wie ir gott gekûndet ward von dem engel Gaberi[ga]el, und sp-
10   richt also, "Der helig engel Gaberi[g]el wart von   Luke 1:26
gott gesendet in ein statt Naseret, zuo einer magt,
die hiess Maria, und was die selb magt gemechelt einem man, der hiess Josep. Und was der
man kûng Davides geschlecht. Und gieng der
15   engel Gaperiel in das hus, da si was an ir heim-
liche, und sprach zuo ir, 'Ave Maria, grazia ple-   (p. 342)
na, *dominus[48] tecum: gott grüs dich, voll gnaden,   Luke 1:28
der herr ist mit dir.' Do Maria dis red er-   Luke 1:29
hort, do erschrak si von dem gruoss und geda-
20   cht, was das were. Do sprach der engel zuo   Luke 1:30
Marien, 'Maria, enförcht dir nit, wan du hast
gnad bi gott funden'"—die gnad die Eva verlorn
hatt in dem paradis vor vil tussent iaren, die
alle gott mit der welt hett gezûrnet—'"und hast
25   du die funden. Sich her, du solt enpfachen und   Luke 1:31
solt geber[n]en einen sun, der sol heissen Iesus.
Dire *wirt[49] gross und fûrnem und wirt geheissen des obresten gottes sun. Und wirt im
gott gen den gewalt her Davides, und wirt
30   sin rich aun end werden.' Do sprach Maria zuo
dem engel, 'Wie mag das beschechen? Ich beken   Luke 1:34

48. daminus
49. wart

On our Lady's Day, as our Lord was announced to her by the angel Gabriel, a sermon:

Ask my Lady that she give me to speak of her praise, to the end that she be praised, and we (5) bettered in soul and in body.

The words that follow are written in the Gospel which we are reading today, and Saint Luke writes us, who was our Lady's special chaplain, and writes us how God was announced to her by the angel Gabriel and (10) says as follows, "The holy angel Gabriel was sent by God to a city by the name of Nazareth, to a virgin, who was named Mary, and this girl was promised in marriage to a man named Joseph. And the man was of King David's house.

And the angel (15) Gabriel went into the house, where she was in her private room, and said to her, 'Ave Maria, gratia plena, dominus tecum: May God greet you, full of grace, the Lord is with you.' When Mary heard these words, she was frightened by the greeting and considered (20) what that might be. The angel then said to Mary, 'Mary, fear not, for you have found grace with God'"—the grace which Eve lost many thousands of years ago in paradise, during which time God was angry with the world—"'and you (25) have found it. Behold, you shall conceive and shall bear a son, who shall be named Jesus. This son will become great and noble, and will be named the son of the highest God. And God will give him lord David's power, and (30) his kingdom will be without end.'

Then Mary said to the angel, 'How can that happen? After all, I as yet know

doch nit manes,'" recht als si welt sprechen,
'Ich han gesetzt in minen sin, das ich iemer aun
man wil sin.' "Do antwirt ir der engel und
35   sprach, 'Der helig geist *kumt[50] zuo dir und des   Luke 1:35
obresten gottes gnad wirt dich umschwetwen,
und da von das kint, das von dir geborn
wirt, das wirt geheissen des obresten gottes   (p. 343)
sun. Und sich zuo einem zeichen, das din nûftel El-

                                                              Luke 1:36
40   lisabet schwanger ist worden an ir alter und hett
nun sechs maunet getragen, wie si doch unber-
heftig was, wan es ist gott nit unmuglich ze   Luke 1:37
tuon.' Do sprach Maria zuo dem engel, 'Sich, ich bin

                                                              Luke 1:38
die gottes dirne. Mir beschech nach dinen wo-
45   rtten.'" Das ist das ewengelium. Do Maria dise
wort gesprach, do enpfieng si zehand gottes
sun und ward des schwanger, und gieng hin
48[51]   zuo Elisabet, die hat sechs manet getragen. Und do sant

                                                              Luke 1:40
Johanes der touffer in siner muotter lip das er-
50   hort, das Maria rett, die gottes schwanger
was worden, und *frouwt[52] sich in siner muotter   Luke 1:41
lip. Und bleip Maria drig manet bi Elisabet,   Luke 1:56
untz das si genas des guotten sant Johanssen, der
do irs suns Iesus vorbott was. Und do Elisabet
55   genas, do gieng Maria wider gen Nasserett,
und schein do offenlich, das si truog. Do gedacht
ir gemachel Josep, das er si weltte lan. Do   Matt. 1:19
erschein im ein engel und hiess in, das er si[53]   Matt. 1:20-21
nit liesse, si wer schwanger worden von dem
60   helgen geist. Und also pflag er ir, untz das si gott   (p. 344)
gebar. Dis hochzit sont wir er[r]en vor allen hoch-

50. kunt
51. die hat written in left-hand margin, marked for insertion after Elisabet
52. fruwt with superscript o above u
53. sich, but ch marked out

no man,'" just as if she had wanted to say, 'I have made up my mind that I always want to be without a man.' "Then the angel answered her and (35) said, 'The Holy Spirit will come to you and the grace of the highest God will overshadow you, and as a result, the child, which is born of you, will be called the son of the highest God. And consider this as a sign of this that your relative (40) Elizabeth has become pregnant at her age and has carried the child for six months now, although she was barren, for it is not impossible for God to do that.' Then Mary said to the angel, 'Behold, I am God's handmaiden. May it happen to me according to your (45) words.'" That is the Gospel.

When Mary spoke these words, she at once conceived God's son and became pregnant with him, and went forth to Elizabeth, who had carried her child for six months. And then Saint (50) John the Baptist heard in his mother's womb what Mary said, who had become pregnant with God, and rejoiced in his mother's womb. And Mary remained with Elizabeth for three months until she bore good Saint John, who was her son Jesus' precursor.

And when Elizabeth (55) gave birth, Mary then went back to Nazareth, and it was then clearly visible that she was with child. Then her intended husband, Joseph, thought that he wanted to leave her. Then an angel appeared to him, and commanded that he not leave her, for she had become pregnant by the (60) Holy Ghost. Thus he cared for her until she gave birth to God.

We shall honor this celebration above all feasts,

zitten, wan es was ein anvang alles guottes und
aller cristner er, wan die welt, die verlorn was
von Adems zitten fûnf tussent iar, mit der wa-
65   rt hûtt [mit] gott versünt. Und an dissem selben
tag wart ouch sant Jacob, sant Johanssen ewengelisten bruoder, das houpt ab geschlagen. Wir
lessent ouch, das an dissem tag und der selben
stund der erst mensch, Adem, und Eva von dem
70   paradis verstossen wurden, das ouch gott mensch was worden in Marien lip. Wir finde̱n
ouch geschriben, das der stund, da Adem den
oupfel aus, das gott an dem crûtz trank essich
und gallen, und der selben stund, do gott de̱n
75   menschen treib uss dem paradis, das er zuo
der selben stund den schacher dar in nam.
Das ist alles beschen an dissem hûttigen tag,
und da von, von der es wegen hût ist beschen, die söllent wir hûtt und iemer lobe̱n.
80   Disser hûtig tag was vor mengem iar bezeichnet und gekûndet von dem wissag Mouses;   (p. 345)
der sach ein böschen, das er vast bran und doch   Exod. 3:2
nit verschwein, und erschein im gott usser dem
böschen. Da bi merken wir, das got wolt von der
85   magt *werden[54] geborn und das doch ir magtuom
nit ward gemindret, wan si was magt vor der
geburt, an der geburt und nach der geburt. Esechiel
sach ein tor, das was allwegent beschlossen und gie-
                                                  Ezek. 44:1-3
ng niemen zuo dem tor uss wan der kûng, und
90   so er da durch gieng, so was es allweg beschlossen.
Das dor, das allwegen beschlossen was, das niemer ward uff getaun, wan so der kûng da durch
wolt gaun, bi dem ist bezeichnet min frouw sant Maria, die nie enkein bekorung enpfieng von ma-

54. werdun

for it was a beginning of everything good and all Christian honor, for the world, which was lost for five thousand years since Adam's time, with that world (65) God was reconciled today. And on this same day Saint James, the brother of Saint John the Evangelist, was beheaded. We also read that on this same day and at the same time as the first human being, Adam, and Eve were turned out of (70) paradise, that God also became man in Mary's womb. We also find written that at the same time when Adam ate the apple, that God drank vinegar and gall on the cross. And at the same time when God drove (75) man out of paradise, that he at the same time admitted the thief into paradise.[28] All of that happened on this day today, and consequently, we shall praise her, Saint Mary, today and forever because of whom it happened today. (80) Precisely this day was indicated and proclaimed many years ago by the prophet Moses; he saw a bush which was brightly burning, but yet wasn't consumed, and God appeared to him out of the bush.

Hereby we note that God wanted to be born of the (85) virgin, and yet her virginity wasn't diminished, for she was a virgin before the birth, during the birth, and after the birth. Ezekiel saw a gate which was always closed and no one went out through the gate save the king, and (90) when he went through it, it always closed. The gate, which was always closed, save when the king wanted to go through, with it is symbolized my Lady Saint Mary, who never experienced[29] any temptation from a man's

28. This would be one of the two men also crucified with Christ.
29. literally 'received'

95   nnes lip. Und also was si mit kûsche beschlossen.
         Wir lessen ouch, das ein kûng, der hiess Nabuchodo-

                                                                    Dan. 3:1

         nosser, der hiess machen ein sul nach eins men-
         [n]schen bilt. Des bildes houpt was guldin, sin brust
         und sin arm warent silberin, sin buch was erin,
100   sin bein isin, sin füss waren irdin. Do dis bilt ge-
         machet ward, do kam ein stein von einem berg,
         den hett niemen an gelan, und lûff an das   (p. 346)
         bilt und zerschluog es, das alles wart zuo
         einem bulver. Und wuochs der stein, das er
105   ward zuo einem grossen steinberg und er
         fult das ertrich. Bi dissem bilt ist bezeichnet
         disse welt; bi menger hand gesmit ist bezeich-
         net menger hand kûngrich, die dire welt
         sint; aber bi dem stein, der da von dem berg
110   viel aun al<le>s anlaun, bi dem ist bezeichnet ûn-
         sser hergott, der da ist ein fest stein; der viel
         von dem berg, das ist, er ward geborn von
          Marien lip, die ein berg ist aller tugent,
         mer denn deheinem menschen, das ie geborn
115   ward. Sechent, also wart dire hûtig tag vor
         geseit in mengen weg, als ich nun e sprach,
         das sin gewalt ist ûber alle rich, wan er ent-   Luke 1:51-52
         setzt, die er wil. Da von lessent wir ein hûb-
         sch bispel. Wir lessent von ûnser frouwen, gottes
120   muotter, do si in empfieng, do sprach si zuo dem
         engel, "Mir müss beschen nach dinen wor-   Luke 1:38
         tten," das si da sprach, "Ma[n]gnifikat. Min sel   Luke 1:46-49
         und min hertz lobet gott, wan er haut ange-   (p. 347)
         sechen min demuot, siner dirnen. Da von wer-
125   dent mich alle geschlecht heissen selig, wan   Luke 1:51-52
         er haut die gewaltigen entsetzt und hett die de-
         mütigen erhöcht"—und lisset man dissen lobsang
         in der vesper. Nun was zuo einem maul ein kû-
         ng, der was also gewaltig und also rich, das in

(95) body. And thus was she closed with chastity.

We also read that a king, who was called Nebuchadnezzar, commanded a statue to be made in a man's image. The statue's head was golden, his breast and his arms were silver, his belly was brass, (100) his legs were iron, his feet were earthen. When the statue was made, a stone came down from a mountain which no one had propelled from there, and it ran against the statue and destroyed it, such that everything was reduced to a dust. And the stone grew until it (105) became a great stone mountain, and it covered the earth.

The statue symbolizes this world. With the metal work by many hands are signified the various kingdoms this world has; but by the stone, which (110) fell from the mountain without having been pushed at all, thereby our Lord God is signified, for he is a solid stone; it fell from the mountain, that is he was born of Mary's body, which is a mountain of all virtues, more than any person who was ever (115) born. See, thus the feast of today was predicted in many ways, as I've already said, that his power is over all kingdoms, for he deposes whomever he wants.

About this we read a nice exemplum: We read about our Lady, God's (120) mother, when she received him, she said to the angel, "May it happen to me according to your words," then she said, "Magnificat. My soul and my heart praise God, for he has seen the humility of me, his handmaiden. Thus (125) all generations will call me blessed, for he has deposed the powerful and has raised up the meek"—and this song of praise is read in the vespers.

Now there was once a king, who was so powerful and so rich, that it

130   dunkt, das in himel noch uff erden im niem-
en gelich wer. Dire kûng reit zuo einem maul
fûr ein kilchen. Da hort er singen ein lop-
sang und hort, das si sungen, "Er entsetzt die ge-
waltigen und erhöcht die demütigen." Do er

135   das erhortt, do sprach er, "Von wem ist das ge-
sungen?" oder wer der were, der in möcht gestossen von sinem gewalt, und sungen si es iemer me, si tetten unrecht. Und also muostent
die paffen des worttes geschwigen, und wenn

140   si kamen an das wort, so muosten si ablaun. Dis
fuogt sich, das der kûng ab siner burg reit in
die statt, die under der burg lag, und gieng
in die batstuben mit vil herschaft und wolt   (p. 348)
baden. Und do er ietz schier hatt gebadet, do kam

145   ein helger engel und gieng usser der batstuben ze aller gliche, als ob er der kûng wer,
und gieng in ein kamer, da des kûngs gewant
was, und leit es an und saus uff des kûngs
ross und reit uff die burg. Und des kûngs ri-

150   tter und knechten wandent alle, das er rechter kûng were, und rittent alle mit im aun
einer, der was in der batstuben bi dem kûng
und pflag sin. Und wist der kûng nit herum.
Wan do er hatt gebadet, do gieng er herus und

155   wolt sich an legen. Do er des kûngs gewand
nit fand, da sprach er, wa sins herren gewannt
wer. Do sprach der bader, sin herr der were
hûtt lang uff die burg und alles sin hofgesint.
Und do das der knecht erhort und das hofge-

160   sind niena sach, do lûff er ouch hin nach und fa-
nt den engel sittzen bi der kûngin mit al-
l[l]en sinen rittern und knechten. Der kûng
lag in der battstuben und was nakent und
ruoft sinen knechten. Und ensprach im nie-   (p. 349)

165   men, wan er was einig in der batstuben.

(130) seemed to him that no one in heaven nor on earth was equal to him. This king once rode past a church. In there he heard the singing of a song of praise and heard that they sang, "He deposes the powerful and elevates the meek."

When he (135) heard that, he said, "About whom is that being sung?" or who would that be who could take his power away from him? And if they would sing it again in the future they would be acting unjustly. And thus the priests had to keep silent as to these words, and whenever (140) they came to these words, they would have to cease.

It came to pass that the king rode down from his castle into the town which lay below the castle, and went to the bathhouse with a great entourage and wanted to bathe. As soon as he had finished bathing, (145) a holy angel came and went out of the bathhouse, entirely looking like the king, and went into a chamber, where the king's clothing was, put it on, sat on the king's stallion, and rode up to the castle.

And the king's (150) knights and servants all thought that he was the real king and all rode with him except for one, who was in the bathhouse with the king, attending to him.

And the king didn't know about it.[30] For when he had bathed, he went out of the room (155) wanting to get dressed. When the servant didn't find the king's clothes, he asked, where his lord's clothing might be. Then the bathhouse owner said that his lord had returned to the castle a long time ago today, and all his retinue.

And when the servant heard that and didn't see (160) the retinue anywhere, he also ran away after them and found the angel sitting next to the queen with all his knights and servants.

The king still lay in the bathhouse, and was naked, and called all his servants, but nobody answered him (165) for he was alone in the bathhouse.

---

30. the deception afoot

Und do er also lag und ruoft, do kam der bader und luogt, was da were. Do sprach der kûng,
*wie[55] si in sust liessen ligen, als er ein buob
were. Do sprach der bader, "Wer bistu oder wer
170 sol din plegen?" Do sprach der kûng, "Du bösswi-
cht, ich bin der kûng, und land mich hie ligen,
und acht min niemen." Do sprach der bader,
"Sprichest du, buob, mir 'böswicht,' wol uss her, oder
ich schlachen dich, das man dich us muoss tra-
175 gen." Der kûng fuor an den bader und wolt in
schlachen. Der bader schluog in, das er da lag. Des
baders knecht nament den kûng bi dem har
und zugent in also nakent fûr die tûr. Also batt
der kûng, das si in liessent ze red komen. Si spra-
180 chen, si weltent einen rechtten böswicht nit hö-
ren reden und wurffent in in das hour und sprachen, ob er sich us geb fûr einen kûng. Do dis die
lût hortten und sachen, do lûffent iung und alt
zuo und wurdent an in werffen. Er lûff   (p. 350)
185 zuo eins ritters hus in der statt, der im
solt der liebst sin, und ruoft, das man in
in liess, es wer der kûng. Do die knecht das
erhortten, do schuttent si wasser uff in und
hiessen in dannen gaun, oder si wurffen in
190 in das *hour,[56] das es ob im ze<sa>men gieng. Er gedacht, wie es es wer ergangen. Und sas der engel uff sinem hus und hort und sach den
spott, den die burger und ire kind mit dem
kûng hatten, und fragt sin ritter, was den
195 lûtten were in der statt, als er nit her
umb wiste. Sin ritter sprachen, "Ein unsiniger
der spreche, er were der kûng ûber die statt
und ûber die burg." Do sprach der engel vil
unkuntlich, "Den sech ich gern. Heissent in

55. bader wie, bader marked out
56. haur; cf. l. 181 above

And as he thus lay there and called out, the bathhouse owner came and looked to see what was going on. Then the king told how they left him lying there, as if he were nothing but a rogue.

The bathhouse owner then said, "Who are you or who is (170) supposed to be attending to you?"

Then the king said, "You rascal, I am the king and they leave me lying here and no one is paying attention to me."

The bathhouse manager then said, "If you, scoundrel, are calling me a rascal, get out or I'll beat you so hard that they'll have to carry (175) you out."

The king charged towards the bathhouse manager and wanted to beat him. The bathhouse manager knocked him down.[31] The servants of the bathhouse manager took the king by his hair and dragged him thus naked outside the door.

In this shape, the king asked the people to let him speak. They said (180) that they didn't want to hear such a real rascal talk, and they threw him into the mud, and asked if he was passing himself off as a king.

When the people heard and saw this, young and old alike ran to the scene and they began to throw things at him. He ran (185) to a knight's house in the city, who was supposed to be dearest to him, and called out to be let in, saying that he was the king.

When the servants heard that, they poured water on him, and commanded him to depart or they would throw (190) him into the mud so much that it would cover him totally. The king considered how all this had happened.

And the angel sat in his house, and heard and saw the mockery to which the citizens and their children subjected the king, and asked one of his knights what was going on (195) with the people in the city, as if he didn't know about it. His knights said, "An idiot is saying that he is the king over the city and the castle."

Then the angel said very ignorantly, "I would love to see him. Have him

31. literally 'hit him that he lay there'

200   her uff gan und hörrent, was er spreche,
        wan er mag wol ein dor sin." Si giengent
        enweg und wurffent im ein hemd an un<u>d</u>
        fuorttent in fûr den *engel.[57] Der engel sass
        bi der kûngin und fragt in, was [mas]

205   mans er were. Er sprach, "Ich enweis, was   (p. 351)
        mans ich bin." Do sprach der engel, "Du machst
        wol ein tor sin. Wan wurd du ie kûng? Dem
        stastu ietz vast ungelich. Du stast einem unsi-
        *nigen[58] torren gelich, wan werestu follen wit-

210   zig, du detest anders also." Do sprach der
        kûng, "Nu enweis ich nit, wie es umb mich er-
        varn ist. Ich was hûtt uff disser burg gewalt-
        iger kûng mit der kûngin, die ietz sitzet ze-
        gegin, und enweis nit, wie es nun ergangen

215   ist, das mich nun hie niemen erkenet." Do spra-
        ch der engel, "Du bist ein tor. Nement und fürent
        in in ein kamer und gebent im ze essen, und ga-
        ng niemen zuo im." Do dire kûng beschlossen
        wart und gaus, do gieng der engel zuo im un<u>d</u>

220   fragt in heimlich, wie es nun wer beschechen
        und ergangen. Do huob er uf[59] und seit von vor-
        nis us,[60] was im wer beschen, und das er aun zwi-
        fel wer rechtter kûng. Do sprach der engel,
        "Du wer[d] der kûng, das ist war, und wer[t]   (p. 352)

225   aber also hochvertig, das du nit woltest, das
        iemen höcher wer *denn[61] du, und woltest
        von hochvart nit lan singen ûnser frouwen
        lopsang, und wertest das in dinem kûng-
        rich. Da von hat dich gott also gedemütiget,

230   das du in erkenest. Ich bin gottes engel und
        bin gesetzt an din statt. Und wiltu dich sel-

57. kûng
58. ngien
59. uf, f badly smeared
60. us, s written over an f
61. wenn

(200) go up here and let us hear what he says, for he may well be a fool."[32] They went away and threw a shirt on him and led him before the angel.

The angel sat next to the queen and she asked him, what kind of a (205) man he might be. He said, "I don't know, what kind of a man I am." Then the angel said, "You may well be a fool. When did you ever become king? You don't resemble him very much. You stand here, resembling more a senseless fool, for if you had all your wits, (210) you would act other than this." Then the king said, "I don't know how it happened to me. Today I was a powerful king at this castle with my queen, who now sits opposite me, and I don't know how (215) it came to pass that no one recognizes me." Then the angel said, "You're a fool. Take him and lead him into a chamber and give him something to eat and let no one come to him."

When this king was locked away and ate, the angel went to him and (220) asked him privately, how it all had happened. He began to speak and told from the beginning how it had happened to him, and that he was doubtlessly the real king. Then the angel said, "You were the king, that is true, but you were (225) so arrogant that you didn't want anyone to be higher than you, and, out of this pride, you didn't allow our Lady's Song of Praise to be sung, and banned it in your kingdom. That is why God has humbled you in this way, (230) that you may acknowledge him. I am God's angel, and have been put in your place. And if you want to recognize yourself

32. He is acting here as if he were ignorant, pretending not to know what he as the angel who had started the whole probe, of course, knew.

ber erkenen und wilt wider keren, das du
gott vor ougen habest und ûnser frouwen lop
bessrist und merist, wan du es habest versu-
235   met, so wil ich dir din kûngrich wider geben,
also[62] das es niemen gewar wirt." Do
sprach der kûng, "Ich bekenn wol, das ich û-
bel gevarn han und das ich gott han erzû-
nt und sin muotter Maria. Das wil ich
240   iemer me gern bessren." Do sprach der *engel,[63]
"Nim hin din gewand und gang zuo *diner[64]
frouwen und zuo dinen lûtten." Und also verschwein der engel und fuor zuo dem, der
in gesant hatt. Der kûng gieng zuo siner   (p. 353)
245   frouwen und zuo sin[n]en rittern, als des
nie gedacht were, und sprach, er hett den
tobigen man enweg gesendet, und sant
botten us in alles sin kûngrich, wa[n] ein
kilch[65] wer, da man ûnser frou-
250   wen lop untz dar geschwigen hette[n], das
man nun sunge zwûrent, und das man
kunte, das gott wer ein kûng, des gewalt
ûber alle kûng were. Also beschach dissem
kûng. Da von erkenent ûch selben und ere-
255   nt die helgen und zevorderst ûnsere frouwen sant Marien, der tag wir hûtt begant.
Wan wer si eret, den wil ir kint eren, der
allemechtig gott. Es spricht sant Johanes
mit dem Guldin Mund von ûnser frouwen,
260   "Als ûns unmuglich ist, das si <ere>[66] dekein menschen, der si mit zwifel an rüffet, als unmuglich ist, das si *dekeinem[67] menschen verziche,

62. a, the top half of the letter l, e and n precede also, all marked out
63. kûng
64. dinen
65. kungl wer kilch, kungl wer marked out
66. The added form ere is suggested by and taken from the Assumption sermon,
l. 129, where the same passage (ascribed here too to John Chrysostom) is used again
in ll.128-133, albeit in a somewhat different German version.

and repent, that you may have God before your eyes and improve and increase our Lady's praise, for you have neglected it, (235) then I will give you back your kingdom in such a manner that nobody will notice it."

Then the king said, "I confess openly that I've done evil, and angered God and his mother Mary. I want to (240) improve on that steadily from now on." Then the angel said, "Take your clothing and go to your (245) lady and your people." And thus the angel vanished and went to him who had sent him.

The king went to his lady and to his knights, as if the matter was entirely forgotten, and said that he had sent the raving man away, and sent messengers out into his entire kingdom, wherever there was a church where they had up to then silenced our (250) Lady's praise, that they should sing it twice from now on, and that they should proclaim that God was a king whose power is over all kings.

Thus it happened to this king. Therefore, recognize yourselves, and (255) honor the saints, and first of all, our Lady Saint Mary, whose day we are celebrating today. For whoever honors her, him her child, almighty God, will want to honor. Saint John with the Golden Mouth says about our Lady, (260) "As it is impossible for us that she honor a human being who calls upon her with doubt, so impossible is it that she should deny any human being

das er si bittet von rechttem lutterm her-   (p. 354)
tzen, wan si heisset und ist vol gnaden."

265   Und da von lobent si hûtt mit dem engelschlichen gruoss und bittent si hûtt mit dem
engelschlichen gruoss, das si mit ûns teile
ir gnad, der si vol ist, und ûns also gebe
ze lebent, das wir an ener welt niemer
270   von ir und irm kint werden gescheiden. Des helffe ûns gott, amen. It<u>em</u>.[68]

---

67. dekeinen

68. It<u>em</u>. This word may indicate that another sermon or item on the Annunciation or a sermon on another feast after March 25, but before April 25, the date
of the next feast (St. Mark) in the Rheinau collection, was to follow. This text may
have been in the exemplar of our copy.

what he asks from her with a just and pure heart, for she is called, and is, 'full of grace'." [33]

(265) And for this reason let us praise her today with the angelic greeting, and ask her today with the angelic greeting, that she share with us her grace, of which she is full, and give us that we may live in such a way that we in the hereafter are never separated (270) from her and her child. May God help us with this, amen.

---

33. Saint John Chrysostom. The quote couldn't be identified.

An sant Marks tag, des ewengelisten, it<u>em</u>: (p. 354)

Dise wort stand geschriben in dem hûttigen
ewengelium, und spricht si santus Markus,
des tag ist hût, und sprach si gott mit sinem
5 götlichen mund, wan wir lessent, das der
guot sant Petter zuo ûnserm herren sprach,
"Herr, wir hand alle ding gelaussen und ha-   Mark 10:29
nd dir nach gevolget." Do sprach ûnser her,
"Werlich, ich sagen ûch, es ist niemen, der du-   Mark 10:30
10 rch minen willen laut sin hus, sinen bruoder[n]
oder sin schwester und vatter und muotter oder   (p. 355)
kint oder aber und matten, er werd es hundert-
valt wider empfachen." Wan gott hett vor gesprochen in dem selben ewengelium, das lichter wer,   Mark 10:25
15 das ein tier schluffe durch einer nadlen öri, denn
das ein rich man kem ze himel. Wan es ist bewert
in mengen weg, das rich lût kum etlich niemer
ze himelrich *kumt.[69] War umb? Ein ieklich rich mensch, der ist eintweder ein sûnder oder eins sûnders
20 erb. Da von sprach er, das es lichter were, ein kem-
eltier durch ein nadel schlûffen, denn ein rich man
kem in gottes rich. Der weg, der da ze himelrich
gatt, der ist gar eng, aber der da gat in die helle,
der ist gar breit und schön. Und ist denn, das du
25 dich geladen hast mit zergenklichem guot, aun zwifel, so machtu den weg bi nûtte gan. Nun merk,
das das guot den menschen nacht und tag bekûmert. Da von spricht ein helg, "Tags so sitzet er und
betrachtet und leit allen fliss dar an, wie er guot
30 gesamne. Also ist er den tag bekûmert. Nachtes
so er schlaffet, [und] so troumt im, wie im es diep   (p. 356)
verstelen." Sich, also ist guot an dire welt recht
als ein torn, wan wa man den torn an grifet ,

69. kunt

On Saint Mark's Day, the Evangelist, another sermon:

These words are written in today's Gospel, and Saint Mark speaks them, whose day it is today, and God spoke them with his (5) divine mouth, for we read that the good Saint Peter said to our Lord, "Lord, we have left everything and have followed you." Then our Lord said, "Truly, I tell you there's no one who for (10) my sake leaves his house, his brother, or his sister and father and mother, or child, or meadow and pasture who will not get it back one hundred times." For God had previously said in the same Gospel that it would be easier (15) for an animal to slip through the eye of a needle than for a rich man to come to heaven. For it is proven in many ways that any rich people scarcely ever come into the Kingdom of Heaven. Why? Every rich person is either a sinner or the inheritor of a sinner. (20) For this reason he said that it would be easier for a camel to slip through a needle than a rich man to come into God's kingdom.

The road that goes to heaven, it's quite narrow, but the one that goes to hell, it's quite wide and beautiful. And in case you've loaded (25) yourself down with transitory goods, without a doubt, you won't be able to make the journey in any way. Now note that man is worried about material goods night and day. That's why a holy man says, "During the day he sits and holds watch and ponders how he might (30) amass material goods. In this manner, he's occupied during the daytime. When he's sleeping at night, he then dreams about how thieves steal it from him." See, material goods in this world are just like a thorn, for when a person grasps the thorn,

35

da sticht er. Also ist es umb das guot: War sich
die richen lût kerent, so sticht si das guot mit gedenken, das si alwegent nach dem guot betrachtent,
wie si es gemerent und wie si es gehalten, wan
in ir hertz *kumt[70] nit ander betrachtung *noch[71] gedenk wan nach guot, als ûnser herr selber spricht,

40

"Wa din guot oder schatz ist, da ist ouch din hertz." Und

Matt. 6:21

da von ist unmuglich, das du nach gott und götlichem leben mugest gedenken, wenn du mit
zitlichem guot bist beladen. Her umb woltent gottes
iunger sich nit mit zergenklichem guot bekûmbren.

45

Und da von lessent wir von dem guotten herren
sant Marko, wie er liess alle ding, die in gottes
und götlichs lebens geirren mochtten, und vol-
gett gott nach. Und wan gott arm was alle die
wil er uff ertrich was, dar umb wolt ouch der

50

guot sant Marcus an dire welt armuot und arbeit han dar umb, das er wirdig wurde des
ewigen lons. Wir lessent von im, das er kam von   (p. 357)
gottes ordnung in Egipttenland und wart da
von den helgen erwelt zuo einem ewengelisten, das

55

er wer der vieren einer, die die *ewengelia[72] sch-
ribent, wan er was der erst, der in den landen brediget, da die lût alwegent abgöt anbettetent. Und
do der guot santus Markus kam zuo einer statt, die
hiess Cirenem, do brediget er da. Und do er da vil zei-

60

chen gettet an siechen, die er gesunt machet, an us<s>et-
zigen, die gereinet wurden, und an *besessnen[73] lûten,
die enbunden wurden von den tûflen, da wart
fil lût bekert von siner lere und wurden getouft.
Do dar nach ward, do ward im kunt getan, das er

65

gen Alexanderia füre und da Cristem brediget, und

70. kunt
71. nach
72. ewengelium
73. bessesnen

it pricks him.

Thus it is with material goods: Wherever (35) rich
people turn, material goods prick them with thoughts, for
no other pondering or thought enters their hearts, except
for their material goods, as our Lord Himself says, (40)
"Wherever your wealth or treasure is, there is also your heart."

That is why it is impossible for you to be able to think
of God and a godly life, if you are laden down with ephemeral
goods. For this reason, God's disciples didn't want to burden
themselves with transitory goods. (45) And therefore we read
of the good man, Saint Mark, how he left all the things which
could lead him astray from God and a godly life and followed
God. And because God was poor all the time he was on earth,
accordingly, the (50) good Saint Mark also wanted to have
poverty and travails so that he became worthy of the eternal
reward.

We read of him that, according to God's will, he came
to Egypt, and there he was chosen from among the saints to
be an evangelist, that (55) he was one of the four who wrote
the Gospels, for he was the first who preached in the countries
where the people worshiped pagan gods in all manners.

And when the good Saint Mark came to a city
named Cyrene, he preached there. And when he did many
(60) miracles there with the sick, whom he made well, with
lepers, who were cleansed, and with possessed people, who
were unbound from the demons, there were many people
converted by his teachings and were baptized. Thereafter it
was made known to him that he (65) should go to Alexandria
and preach Christ there, and

uff der statt do bereit er sich und fuor enweg. Do fuogt
sich, das er kam gen Alexander<ia>. Und do er also gieng, do brach im ein riem an sinem schuoch. Do sprach er, "Ich weis wol fûr war, das min vart sol
70   verricht werden, und enmag mich der tûfel
nit erwenden," und sach einen sutter da sitzen
und gap im sinen schuoch ze machen. Und do der   (p. 358)
sutter den [schuoch ze machen und do der sutter
den] schuoch wolt machen, do stach er sich ûbel
75   in die linken hand und schrei, "Ach, gott!" Do das
der guot sant Markus erhort, do sprach er,
"Werlich, min vart wil verricht werden
und nûtz," und spei an die erden und macht ein
hörwili und salbet dem sutter sin hand in
80   dem namen ûnsers herren Iesus Cristus. Do
ward der sutter gesund an siner hand uff
der statt. Do der sutter sach den grossen gewalt, den santus Mark[a]us haut an sin[d]er hant ge-
zögt, do sprach er zuo im, "Ich bitt dich, gottes kne-
85   cht, das du komest in min hus und mit mir
essest, wan du hast din erbermd mit mir hût
geteilt." Do sprach sant Markus, "Gottes segen
sige in dissem hus," und sprach frölich, "Gott
gebe dir das himelsch brot." Also nam in der
90   sutter und fuort in in sin hus. Und do er sin gebett sprach, und gar frölich sassen, do sprach
der sutter, "Lieber gottes knecht, wennen
bist oder wennen *kumst,[74] oder wer git dir   (p. 359)
den grossen gewalt, *den[75] din[n]e wort hant?" Do
95   sprach santus Markus, "Ich bin ûnsers herren gottes knecht, Iesus Cristus, des lebenden gottes
sun." Do sprach der sutter, "Den sech ich gar gern."
Do sprach santus Markus, "So wil ich dich in lassen
sehen." Und begund santus Markus dem sutter

74. kunst
75. die

immediately, he prepared himself and departed.

It then came to be that he went to Alexandria, and on his way there, a strap broke on his shoe. Then he said, "I certainly know that my trip will (70) be accomplished and the devil can't turn me away," and saw a cobbler sitting there and gave him his shoe to be repaired. And when the cobbler wanted to repair the shoe, he pricked himself (75) on his left hand and cried out, "Oh, God!"

When the good Saint Mark heard that, he said, "Truly, my trip will be completed and useful," and spat on the ground and made an ointment out of saliva and earth and used it as a salve on the cobbler's hand in (80) the name of our Lord Jesus Christ.[34] Then the cobbler's hand was healed immediately.

When the cobbler saw the great power which Saint Mark had shown on his hand, he said to him, "I ask you, God's servant, (85) to come to my house and eat with me, for you shared your compassion with me today." Then Saint Mark said, "May God's blessing be in this house," and said cheerfully, "May God give you heavenly bread."[35]

Thus the (90) cobbler took him by his hand into his house. And when he said his prayer and they sat down cheerfully, the cobbler said, "Dear servant of God, where do you come from, or who gives you the great power which your words have?" Then (95) Saint Mark said, "I am a servant of our Lord Jesus Christ, son of the living God." Then the cobbler said, "I'd be very happy to see him." Then Saint Mark said, "So I will let you see him."

And Saint Mark began

34. The manner in which Saint Mark heals the cobbler closely parallels Christ's healing of the blind man in the Gospel of John 9:6.

35. This is probably the Eucharist after his conversion, which is to occur soon, or the bread in heaven after a Christian's death.

100   bredigen und von gott sagen, das er wer ge-
          war gott, von dem er rette, und seit im, was
          die wisagen von im geschriben hatten. Der su-
          tter geloupt alles das, das im santus Markus
          seit, und ward getouft, er und alles sin gesint,
105   und ander lûtten vil, die da warent zegegin,
          die wurdent all glöbig. Und do wart an dem
          helgen ostertag, do ir ostertag was, do sam-
          natten sich die iuden und ander ungelöbig lût
          und santen specher, die in suochtten. Und do[76] si in
110   suochtten, do fundent si in ligen an sinem gebet
          und nament ein seil und bundent im es umb
          sin kellen und zugent in hin und her. Und do
          si in also zugen, do lopt er sinen schöpfer und
          sprach also, "Min lieber herr gott, Iesus Cristus,   (p. 360)
115   ich sagen dir dank und lop, das du mich dar
          zuo hast benempt, das ich dis lit durch dinen
          willen." Und sin fleisch, das hanget lang uff de_m_
          ertrich, und warent die stein und die erd rot
          von bluot, das von sinem lip floss. Und do an de_m_
120   abent ward, do gehielten si in in *einem[77] ker-
          ker untz mornendes und nament in aber
          her uss und bunden im aber ein seil an sin ke-
          len und zugent in an die strassen. Und do si
          in also zugent, do lopt der guot santus Markus
125   ûnsern herren und sprach, "Ich enpgilch dir, herr,
          min[n]en geist in din hend." Und do er das gespr-
          ach, do schied sin helge <sel> von sinem lip. Dis hand
          wir hût gelessen von dem guotten herren sant
          Marko. Nun sechent wir wol und wissent es
130   ouch, das die helig cristenheit ein selige gewon-
          heit hett, das si hût gaut mit crûtz und hût va-
          stet fûr den gechen tod. Und dire tag heiset

---

76. o of do is written superscript over an unidentifiable letter which has been
blackened out.
    77. einen

(100) to preach to the cobbler and spoke of God, that he was the true God, of whom he was talking, and told him what the prophets had written about him. The cobbler believed all of that which Saint Mark said to him and was baptized, he and all of his company, (105) and many other people who were present there; they all became believers.

And when it turned Holy Easter, when it was their Easter day, the Jews assembled and other unbelievers and sent spies to seek him out. And when they (110) sought him, they then found him at prayer, and took a rope, and tied it around his neck and pulled him back and forth.

And when they thus pulled him, he praised his Creator and said as follows, "Lord God, Jesus Christ, (115) I give you thanks and praise, that you have called me to suffer this pain for your sake." And his body lingered for a long time on the ground, and the stones and the earth were red from the blood which flowed from his body.

And when it became (120) evening, they held him in a prison until the following morning and took him outside again and tied another rope around his neck and pulled him onto the street. And when they thus pulled him, the good Saint Mark praised (125) our Lord and said, "I commend to you, Lord, my spirit into your hands." And when he had said that, his holy soul departed from his body.

We read this today concerning the good man Saint Mark. Now we see it well, and know it (130) too, that holy Christianity has a blessed custom, that believers go around today with the cross and fast concerning a sudden death.[36] And this day is called

---

36. that is, on the Feast of Saint Mark

ein betttag dar umb, das wir gott bitten um<b>
ûnser notdurft, und da von so merkent, wa
135   von sich das erhaben habe. Wir lessent, das eins   (p. 361)
mals das ertrich also tûrr was, das es nit mo-
cht bern noch frucht bringen, und das die lût
und vich alles nider viel und starb, und das
die beren und die wolf vil lûtten verdarptten
140   und dik giengen in die stett und zerzartten
die iungen kint. Dar umb wart gesetzt, das
man vasteti und gienge mit crûtz und ouch bet-
teti[n]. Das erhort gott ze hand und wurdent
guotte zit in allen dingen. So lessent wir, das dire
145   hûtig tag dar umb gesetzt ist ze fasten. Ein wasser heisset die Diener und rint bi Rom. Das was
also gross wider sin gewonheit, das es in die stat
gieng und warf in der statt nider vil kilchen
und hûser mit lûtten und erdrankt si. Und in dem
150   selben wasser kam ein grosser trak gerunen
mit vil andern wûrmen und warf si das
wasser an den stad und sturben. Und kamen von
wûrmen als grosser gesmak und unreinikeit,
das die lût nider viellen[78] und sturben. Und sach
155   man komen schoss von himel an die lût, und
wen die traffen, die sturben aun underlaus an   (p. 362)
der statt, und starb der baubst Peleigen. Dar nach
starp das volk von Rom vil nach alles sament. Do wart ein babst, der hiess Gregorius. Der
160   manet die lût, das si vastetten und betteten
und das crûtz trügen. Do das volk das gedet,
do hort das ûbel alles sament. Und da von
ward gesetzt, das man den selben tag, als hût
ist, sol vasten mit crûtzgang und betten, das
165   ûns gott behuott vor dem gechen tod und ûns
ûnser *vich[79] beschirm. Und wan dik dis zittes von

78. viellen, with the first e of viellen written superscript over the i
79. ûch
80. kunt

a day of prayer for the reason that we ask God about our needs, and therefore note well, (135) how this came into being.

We read that once there was such a drought on earth, that it couldn't bear nor produce fruit, and the people and all the livestock fell down and died, and that the bears and wolves killed many people (140) and often went into the cities and tore the young children to pieces. For this reason it was established that people should fast and have processions with the cross and should also pray. God heard this prayer immediately and good times in every respect returned.

Thus we read that (145) today was accordingly established as a day to fast. A river is named Tiber and it flows past Rome.[37] And it was so swollen against its nature that it flowed into the city and, in the city, knocked down many churches and houses with people and drowned them. And in the (150) same water, a huge dragon came swimming with many other serpents, and they threw the water up over the bank and died.[38] And from the serpents there came such a great stench and uncleanliness, that the people fell down and died. And (155) bolts from the sky were seen coming towards the people, and whomever they struck, they died immediately then and there, and also Pope Pelagius died.[39] After that almost the whole population of Rome died.

Then a man named Gregory became the pope. He (160) admonished the people to fast, pray, and carry the cross. When the people did that, the evil ceased all together. And for this reason it was established that on the same day as today is, people should fast with processions of the cross and pray that (165) God may protect us from a sudden death and shield our livestock. And because it often happens at this time

37. Apparently, the German word 'Diener' here is an incorrect spelling of Tiber.
38. on the city-side of the river
39. This was apparently an epidemic.

unwetter *kumt,[80] das die frucht disser zit verderben wil, so ist gesetzt, das wir mit crûtz
gangen und ûns u[i]eben mit vasten und mit
170   betten an dissem tag, das gott ûns und ûnser
*vich[81] und den ertwuocher beschirm. Da von so si-
nt hût erst hastig an dem gebett und an dem
vassten, wan wes wir hût gott bitten mit gemeinem gebett, das wil ûns gott erhören.

175   Wan es spricht sant Bernhart, "So vil lût zesamen *kumt[82] ze betten, die werdent stark
an ir gebett, und ist unmuglich, das vil lû-
ttes gebett nit erhört werde." Bettent fûr   (p. 363)
enander, das wir behaltten werden, wan
180   des gerechtten menschen flissiges gebett ist
gar guot. Wan wir lessent, das Helias was
als ûnser eins tötmûg, das er das volk nit
mocht bekeren von ir ungelouben, und batt

1 Kings 18:20-39

gott, das in drin iaren nie regen kam uff
185   ertrich. Und in drin manotten, do die arbeit
das volk an gieng, do bekertten si sich zuo gott. Do
batt er aber gott, und wart regnen, und gap
das ertrich frucht. Nun wil ich ûch sagen ein
kurtz bispel von gebett. Es was ein guott ein-
190   sidel, der lag in einem walt an seinem gebett,
und sant der keisser[83] Iulianus ein-
en tûfel, der im zehant ein bottschaft endete.
Und kam der tûfel zuo des einsidels hus und
wolt da fûr varn. Under danen da lag der
195   einsitel an sinem gebett, und da von mocht
der tûfel nit fûr in komen and muost da an
der statt zwenzig tag stan, wan die wil bettet der einsidel. Und do der keisser fragt, wa

81. ûch
82. kunt
83. After der, the scribe wrote tûfel einen, marked it out, then continued with
keisser.

because of bad weather, that the crop of this season will be
destroyed, so it is established that we go on processions with
the cross and apply ourselves to fasting and (170) praying on
this day in order that God may protect us and our livestock
and the fruits of the earth.

For this reason, be especially intent today on prayer
and fasting, for what we all ask, praying together, that God
will hear and grant us. (175) For Saint Bernard says, "When
many people come together to pray, they become strong
in their prayer, and it is impossible for the prayer of many
people not to be heard."

Pray for one another that we may be preserved,
for (180) the ardent prayer of a righteous person is highly
effective. For we read that Elijah, as we all, was so dead tired
that it was impossible for him to convert the people from
their unbelief, and he asked God never to let it rain on earth
for three years. (185) And in three months, when hardship hit
the people, they converted to God. Then he asked God again,
and it started to rain and the earth bore fruit.

Now I want to tell you a short tale about prayer.
There was once a good (190) hermit, who, in a forest, lay at
his prayer, and the Emperor Julian sent a devil, who should
deliver a message to him at once. And the demon came to
the hermit's house and wanted to approach him there. In the
meantime, the (195) hermit lay there at his prayer, and for
that reason, the demon could not get to him and had to stand
there twenty days on the spot, for during that time the hermit
prayed. And when the emperor asked where

er also lang were gesin, do sprach er, "Dört   (p. 364)
200   lag ein mû<n>ch an sinem gebett also ernstlich,
       das ich da stuond zwenzig tag. Do beittet ich,
       ob er des gebettes ein ent wölt machen. Do
       gap er im nit endes, do mocht ich ouch nit
       fûr komen vor sinem gebett, und da von
205   kum ich, das ich die botschaft nit geendet
       han." Do trouwt im Iulianus, was er im ma-
       rtter welt an tuon. Und fuor Iulianus an ein-
       en strit und wart da erschlagen und fuor
       in die ewigen helle. Nun merkent, wie
210   stark des einsitels gebett was, das er den
       tûfel behuop mit sinem gebett, das er wed-
       er in den lûfften noch under der erden noch
       niena fûr mocht komen. Und aus und trank
       der selb mensch als ûnser eins. Do was aber
215   sin hertz also mit got vereint, das im alles
       das lon bracht, das er dett, als sant Paulus sp-
       richt, "Wir essent, wir trinkent, oder was   1 Cor. 10:31
       wir tuond, das tuon wir *alles[84] in gottes namen."
       Der gott minnet, was der guotes tuot, das *ku-   Rom. 8:28
220   mt[85] im alles ze nutz. Da von flissent ûns, das   (p. 365)
       wir sigen in gottes dienst, das ist, das wir
       sigen[86] aun totsûnd. Was wir denn tügent, das
       *kumt[87] ûns alles ûnser sele ze nutz, und wil ûns
       gott erhören, was wir in bitten mit ernst. Nun
225   bitten wir den guotten herren sant Marko, das
       er hûtt ûnser fûrsprech sige gegen got des wir
       in bitten umb ûnser noturft, und ûns beschirm
       sel und lip und guot und des wir leben söllen.[88]

84. als
85. kunt
86. sigen in: in marked out
87. kunt
88. The o of söllen carries a superscript o rather than the expected e.

he had been for so long, he said, "A monk (200) lay there at his prayer so earnestly, that I stood there for twenty days. I waited for him to finish his prayer. Since he didn't finish it, I also couldn't approach him because of his praying, and that is why (205) I come to tell you I didn't accomplish the mission." Then Julian threatened him with all kinds of torture. And Julian went into a battle, and was killed there, and went into eternal hell.

Now note how (210) strong the prayer of the hermit was, that with his prayer he prevented the devil from coming closer so that he could proceed neither from above, nor from below, nor from anyplace else. And this person ate and drank, as we do. But (215) his heart was then so one with God that anything he did brought him reward, as Saint Paul says, "Whether we eat or drink, or whatever we do, let us do all that in God's name." If one loves God, whatever good this person does, it all comes (220) to his own benefit. Let us apply ourselves to be in God's service, that is to say, that we may be without deadly sin. Whatever we then do, all that comes to the benefit of our soul, and God will hear us and grant us, whatever we seriously ask him. Now (225) let us ask the good lord Saint Mark, that he today be our advocate before God in what we ask him about our needs, and that he may protect for us our soul and body and the good things, and also our future livelihood.

An sant Petters und sant Paulus tag, item: (p. 389)

Dise wort stant in dem ewengelium, das man
hût lisset, und sprach si ûnser her, do er ûff
ertrich gieng, zuo dem guoten herren sant Pe-
5   tter, des tag wir hût begand in der helgen
cristenheit. Der guot gott sprach also, "Du bist   Matt. 16:18
ein vestes fûlment aller der cristenheit, und
was du bindest uff ertrich, das ist gebunden   Matt. 16:19
in himelrich, und was du enbindest uff ert-
10   rich, das ist enbunden in himelrich völlenklich."
An disen wortten merkent wir, das gott dem
guotten sant Petter gap den gewalt, das er bu-
nde und enbunde den menschen von den
sûnden, und wem er uff ertrich vergep sin
15   sûnd, das dem gott si well vergen in dem himelrich. Disen selben gewalt hett er den prie-
stern allen geben. Und welte die cristenheit   (p. 390)
gott umb kein ding lopen, si sölte nit laussen,
si sölt in dar umb lopen, das er den gewalt
20   uff ertrich haut gelaussen, das enkein mensche
so sûndig ist, wil es abkomen siner sûnd, so vin-
det er die priester an sant Petters statt, die
im sin sûnd vergent. Sit wir nun hût begangen
des guotten herren sant Petters tag, so wil
25   ich ûch von im sagen sin leben, das ir in dester
gerner erent mit allen guotten werken, wan
er ist ein fûrst aller helgen. Wir lessent also, das
sant Petter was von Betsaida und was sant Anderes bruoder und was von sinen frûnden ge-
30   heissen Simon und was ze Gal<i>lea; da was er ein
vischer. Und do er und sin bruoder, der guot herr

118

On Saint Peter's and Saint Paul's Day, another sermon:

These words are to be found in the Gospel which
is read today, and our Lord spoke them, when he went on
earth to the good lord Saint (5) Peter, whose day we celebrate
today in holy Christendom. Good God thus spoke, "You are
a strong foundation for all of Christianity, and whatever you
bind on earth, that is bound in heaven, and whatever you
release on (10) earth, that is completely released in heaven."

In these words we note that God gave good Saint
Peter the power to bind and unbind man from sin, and to
whomever he forgives his (15) sins on earth, that God wants
to forgive him in the kingdom of heaven. He gave this same
authority to all priests. And if Christianity wanted to praise
God for anything, it shouldn't fail to praise him for leaving
this power (20) on earth, that no man is so sinful, that, if he
wants to get rid of his sins, he finds priests in Saint Peter's
place, who forgive him his sins.[40]

Since we're celebrating today the feast of the good lord
Saint Peter, I want (25) to tell you about his life, that you all
the more eagerly honor him with all good works, for he is a
prince of all saints.[41] Thus we read about him that Saint Peter
lived in Bethsaida and was Saint Andrew's brother, and was
(30) called Simon by his friends, and was in Galilee. There he
was a fisherman. And when he and his brother, the good lord

40. the so-called 'Schlüsselgewalt' or 'Power of Keys'
41. Latin 'princeps' = originally 'the first'

sant Anderes, zuo einem mal vischeten, do gieng
ûnser herr bi des mers stad und sprach zuo in,
"Venite, koment nach mir. Ich wil usser ûch ma-   Matt. 4:19
35   chen vischer, das ir lût vachent." Do si das erhortten, do liessent si das schiff und das netz und
volgetten gott nach, er und sin bruoder, und also
wurdent si gottes iunger und sin vischer, wan
si hant in diser bittren welt mengen gro-   (p. 391)
40   ssen sûnder gevangen und bekert mit dem netz der helgen ler, wan si hant meng mensche
gezogen in das himelrich. Dire helg sant Petter,
der was allwegent ûnserm herren sunder heim-
lichen denn kein ander zwölf bot und minet
45   ouch gott ernstlicher denn die andren. Und do ûnser herr zuo einem mal kam ze Sarigen, do fragt   Matt. 16:13
er den guotten sant Petter, was die lût von im
retten, und ouch die andern iunger, oder wen
si sprechen, wer er were. Und die iunger ant-
50   wirtten und sprachen, "Etwer spricht, du sigest   Matt. 16:14
Helias; so spricht etwer, du sigest sant Johanes, der
touffer; etlich Ierumiges oder etlich einen wissagen."
Do sprach ûnser herr, "Wen iechent aber ir, der ich
                                     Matt. 16:15
sige?" Do antwirt im sant Petter und sprach, "Du bi-
                                     Matt. 16:16
55   st des lebendes gottes sun, Iesus Cristus." Do sprach
ûnser herr, "Petter, du bist selig, wan das bluot noch
                                     Matt. 16:17
das fleisch geoffnet dir es nie. Min vatter von
himel haut dir es geoffnet, der da in dem him-   Matt. 16:17
el ist, und da von so wandel ich dinen namen   Matt. 16:18
60   und heiss dich Petter,"—das ist als vil gesprochen
als ein vestes *fûlemunt[89]—"dar uf ich wil setzen mi-   (p. 392)
nen gewalt," recht als er spreche, minen ge-
walt gip ich dir. Wen du uff ertrich von sinen   Matt. 16:19

89. fûlemût

Saint Andrew, were once fishing, our Lord walked along the
seashore and said to him, "Venite, follow me. I want to make
(35) fishermen out of you, that you catch men."

When they heard that, they left the boat and the net
and followed God, he and his brother, and thus they became
God's disciples and his fishermen, for in this bitter world they
caught and converted many (40) great sinners with the net
of their holy teaching, for they pulled many men into the
kingdom of heaven. This holy Saint Peter was always closer
to our Lord than any other apostle, and Saint Peter also loved
(45) God more earnestly than the others.

And when our Lord once came to Caesarea, he asked
good Saint Peter, what the people said about him, and also
the other disciples, or who they said he was. And the disciples
(50) answered, saying, "Some say, you are Elijah; on the other
hand, some say you're Saint John, the Baptist; some Jeremiah
or some a prophet." Then our Lord said, "But who do you say
I am?" Then Saint Peter answered him, "You are (55) the son
of the living God, Jesus Christ."

Our Lord then said, "Peter you are blessed because
neither blood nor flesh ever revealed this to you. My Father
from heaven revealed it to you, and therefore I change your
name (60) and call you Peter,"—that means as much as a
strong foundation—"whereupon I will place my power," just
as if he were saying, my authority I give to you. Whomever
you on earth unbind from his sins

sûnden enbindest in der bicht mit dem aplaus, de<u>m</u>
65   wil ich vergen all sin sûnd und wil im geben das
himelrich, und wen du nit enbindest von sinen
sûnden, dem wil ich ouch nit vergen sin sûnd. Den
[den] gewalt gab gott dem guotten sant Petter un<u>d</u>
sinen nachkomnen. Ach, wie selig der mensch
70   ie ward geborn, dem gott so grossen gewalt gab
oder git. Und do in gott wolt der helgen cristenheit geben zuo einem lerer, do wolt er[90] in lassen
vallen in anvechtung und in arbeit, das er
dem sûnder dest bas geloupen möcht und sich û-
75   ber si erbarmen. Und da von lessen wir, das dar
nach, do got wolt liden die marter durch der
welt heil willen, do sprach er zuo sine<u>n</u> iungern,   Matt. 26:31
das si sin der nacht all wurden lögnen. Do sprach   Matt. 26:35
sant Petter, er wölt mit im gan an den dod; do   Matt. 26:34
80   sprach ûnser her<u>r</u>, er wurt sin vor hanenkra dri
stunt verlögnen, also es ouch ergieng. Und do man
ûnser<u>n</u> here<u>n</u> also gar ûbel handelt, do stuond der   Luke 22:55
guot herr sant Petter bi einer gluot und warmd sich.
Do fragt in ein frouw, ob er ouch Iesus iunger wer.   (p. 393)
                                                   Mark 14:67
85   Do *schûwt[91] er, das er sin nût bekande und lögnet sin
                                          Mark 14:68-72
also zuo drin mallen vor hanenkrat. Sechent, dar
umb verhangt gott über den guotten sant Petter,
das er in als gross sûnd viel, das er ouch kûnt erbermt han gegen dem sûnder. Und dar umb, das
90   wir dester besser sicherheit und zuoversicht haben,
so merkent, das sich gott nach siner urstende sant
Petter offneti e denn keinem zwölfbotten. Un<u>d</u> wo<u>n</u>
                                         John 21:15-18
er in dristund *vragt,[92] ob er in ût minnette, do sprach

90. lower portion of letter d precedes er
91. schouwt, o and t superscript
92. vargt

in confession with the absolution, him (65) I will forgive
all his sins and will give him the kingdom of heaven, and
whomever you do not unbind from his sins, I also will not
forgive his sins. God gave this power to good Saint Peter and
his successors. Oh, how blissfully the person (70) was ever
born, to whom God gave or gives such great authority!

And when God wanted to give him to holy
Christendom as a teacher, he let him fall into temptation and
travail, that he might all the better identify with the sinners
and have (75) mercy with them.

And therefore we read that afterwards, when God
wanted to suffer death for the sake of the world's salvation,
our Lord said to his disciples, that during the night all of
them would forsake him. Then Saint Peter said that he
wanted to go with him unto death; upon (80) which our Lord
said that he would deny him three times before the cock's
crow, as it also happened.

And when they treated our Lord so very badly,
the good lord Saint Peter then stood by a glowing fire and
warmed himself. Then a woman asked him whether he was
a disciple of Jesus, too. (85) Then he dodged the question,
saying that he didn't know him, and thus denied him three
times before the cock's crow.

See, for this reason, God let it happen to good Saint
Peter that he fell into such great sin, that he also knew how
to have compassion with the sinner. And to the end that
(90) we feel more safe and confident, notice, that after his
resurrection, God revealed himself to Saint Peter before any
other apostle. And when he asked him three times if he loved
him,

sant Petter, "Herr, du weist wol, das ich dich minne̱n."

95   Do enpfalch im gott, das er sin schaf fuorte, das ist, sin

John 15:17

cristenheit spiste mit der gottes ler, und tet im ku̱nt,
das er ouch den tod solt liden an dem crûtz. Und do ûnser herr ze himel fuor, do bredget der guot sant Petter
offenlich von gott und aun vorcht, wie er e die einig-

100   en iunkfrouwen vorcht. In dem selben zit was einer
ze Rom, der hiess Simon, und was ein zouberer; der hat

Acts 8:9-10

die lût[93] vil betrogen mit sinem zouber[er]. Und do er sach,
das die zwölfboten und die si bekerten, das die de̱n
helgen geist hatten enpfangen und kunden reden

105   allerhant sprachen—zwo und sibenzig sprache̱n—, do bracht Simon, der zouberer, dem guotten here̱n sant Pe-

Acts 8:19

ter gross guot, das er im hulfe des, das er ouch das   (p. 394)
möcht getuon. Do sprach sant Petter, "Din guot sig

Acts 8:20

mit dir in dem ewigen tod." Und von dem selbe̱n

110   wort, "Wer geistlich gap verkouft oder kouft, der
tuot totsûnd." Und von dem tag, do gestiess der
zouberer sant Pettern nie ûbels ab und sprach,
sant Petter, der wer ein trieger und gep aber
sich selp us fûr cristen, das er gott wer. Und do

115   Simon der zouberer die lût ze Rom gar verkert,
do begunt sant Petter eins tags mit im kriege̱n.
Under danen da truog man einen totten ze grap,
und sprach Simon zuo den lûtten, "Was marter
wend ir disem Petter antuon, ob ich disen totten

120   heiss uff stan?" Do sprachen si, "Wir wellen in verbrenen." Do gebot Simon dem tûfel, das er in ruor-
te, als er lebte. Do das die lût sachen und horten,
do lobten si Simon und sprachen, sant Petter wer
ein trieger. Do sprach sant Petter, "Wer, das diser

93. lût superscript over the space between die and vil

Saint Peter said, "Lord, you know well that I love you." (95) Then God entrusted to him to feed his sheep, that is, that he nourished his Christians with Christ's teachings, and announced to him that he should also suffer death on the cross. And when our Lord went up to heaven, good Saint Peter preached openly about God and without fear, however much he was afraid before of that one (100) young woman.

At the same time there was someone in Rome named Simon, who was a sorcerer; he had deceived the people much with his magic.[42] And when he saw that the apostles and those they converted had received the Holy Spirit and could speak (105) all kinds of languages—seventy-two languages—Simon the sorcerer brought great wealth to the good lord Saint Peter in order for him to help him that he could do that, too.

Saint Peter then said, "May your wealth be with you in eternal death." And from the same (110) word we have the doctrine, "Whoever buys or sells spiritual matters, he commits a deadly sin."

And from that day, the sorcerer never kept evil away from Saint Peter, and said that Saint Peter was a fraud, but passing himself off for a Christian, even for God himself. And when (115) Simon the sorcerer was totally leading the people in Rome astray, one day Saint Peter began to oppose him.

At that time a dead man was carried to his grave, and Simon said to the people, "To what kind of torment do you want to subject this Peter, if I command this dead man (120) to arise?" Then they said, "We will burn him on a pyre."

Then Simon ordered the devil to touch him, giving the effect that he was alive. When the people saw and heard that, they praised Simon and said that Saint Peter was a charlatan. Saint Peter then said, "If this

42. Lines 106-109 basically parallel information (cf. notes in German text) written in the Acts of the Apostles 8:9-20. Further material on Simon in this sermon (lines 110-186 in the German text) is not based on biblical scripture.

125   tot<e> lebte, so stuont er uff und rette; wan er aber dis
        nit getuon mag, so sond ir wissen, das es *kumt[94] von
        dem tûfel." Do das das volk erhort, do wolten si
        in zwingen, das er den totten uff hiess stan. Do
        wolt er in sin endrunen. Do viengen si in und wol-
130   ten in han verbrent. Do batt sant Petter, das   (p. 395)
        man in liess genessen. Darnach seit er, wie er
        was vor einem richter und in sant Petter erbat.
        Do si das hortten, do lopten si in all gemeinlich
        und veriagtent den zouberer. Do was einer da,
135   der hiess Marzellius, der was des *zouberers[95] wirt
        gesin. Der wolt in nit me laden und luot sant
        Pettern in sin hus. Do gieng Simon der *zouberer[96]
        zuo und nam einen grossen hunt und band den
        in das selb hus hinder die dûr und wolt da
140   mit sant Pettern von der herberg triben. Do
        gieng sant Petter und erkant den hund und
        gebout im, das er niemen bisse und an Simon
        lûffe und in schante. Also lûff der hunt an Simon
        under den lûtten und warf in nider und brach
145   im sin[97] gewand zuo kleinen stûklin. Und floch
        der zouberer und lûff uss der statt, und lûff im
        nach hunt und kint. Und verbarg sich zwei iar,
        und kam do zuo dem keisser Nero und sprach, das
        er gott were, und sprach, sant Petter und sant Pau-
150   lus werent Römern vigent und werent inen
        unnûtz. Do sant der keiser nach innen, und do si
        kamen, do bewarten si wol *vor[98] dem keiser, das   (p. 396)
        Simen ein trieger wer und das Cristus richsnet
        in siner gotheit. Do sprach Simon, er welte beweren,
155   das er gott were und hiess im machen einen hoch-
        en durn, von dem er ze himel füre, und sprach, er

94. kunt
95. zuofers
96. zuberer, with superscript o over u
97. sin hu, hu marked out
98. von

(125) dead man were alive, he would stand up and talk; but because he can't do this, you should know that it comes from the devil."

When the people heard that, they wanted to force him[43] to command the dead man to stand up. Then he wanted to run away from them. But then they caught him and (130) wanted to have him burned up. Saint Peter then asked them to let him go unharmed. He told later that he appeared before a ruler, and Saint Peter pleaded to let him go.

Then they all praised him with one voice and chased off the sorcerer. Then there was a man (135) named Marzellius, who had been the sorcerer's landlord. He didn't want to invite him in any more and invited Saint Peter into his house.

Simon the sorcerer then went and took a big dog and bound it in the same house behind the door, and wanted (140) to drive Saint Peter from the lodging with it. Saint Peter then went and treated the dog in a friendly manner and commanded it that it bite no one but rather run and attack Simon and bring him to shame.

Thus the dog ran at Simon among the people and threw him down and tore[44] (145) his clothing into tiny pieces. And the sorcerer fled and ran out of the city, and dogs and children ran after him. And he hid for two years, and then came to the Emperor Nero, and said that he was God and that Saint Peter and Saint Paul (150) were enemies of the Romans and of no use to them. Then the emperor sent for them, and when they came, they proved clearly before the emperor that Simon was a charlatan, and that Christ reigned in his divinity.

Then Simon said he wanted to prove (155) that he was God and had himself a high tower made, from which he would go up to heaven, and said he

---

43. presumably Simon, once again

sölte nit von den sûndern ze himel varn. Do hiess
der keiser Nero, das man im zehant machte einen
hûbschen turn, von dem er ze himel füre. Do der
160   turn gemacht wart, da kam alles das volk dar
von Rom ze luogen. Und kam Simon gekrönt und
gieng uf den turn und begund fliegen, und fuor-
tten in die tûfel in den luft. Do sprach der keiser
zuo den zwölfbotten, "Ir sint ûberwunden, sechent
165   ir nit, wie er in den himel vert?" Do sprach sant
Petter, "Nun beittent ûns ein klein wil, so werden
ir sechen, das wir recht habent, und alles, das
er tuot, das tuot er mit des tûfels rat." Do sprach
Nero, "Ir sint noch in ûwerm glouben. Sechent ir
170   nût, wa er hin vert?" Do sach sant Petter sant Paulus
an. "Paule," sprach er, "sich hin zuo Simon." Do huop sant
Paulus sin houpt uf und luogt und sach den zouberer an und sach *in[99] fliegen. Do sprach er zuo sant
Pettern, "Petere, wes beitestu, war umb tuostu nit,   (p. 397)
175   was du tuon wilt?" Do hort der keiser, was si mit
enander retten, und lachet und sprach, "Dis sachent,
das si ûberwunden sint, und beginent nun tore_n_."
Do sprach sant Petter zuo dem keiser, "Nun wirstu sechen, das wir nit toren sint." Do sprach sant Pau-
180   lus zuo sant Petter, "Tuo, was du wilt tuon, ze hant."
Do sach sant Petter uff gegen Simon und sprach,
"Ich beschwer ûch tûfel, die da fürent den zouberer, der da mengen menschen betrogen ha[n]t, das
ir in lassent vallen und ir in fûr dis mal nit
185   me fürent." Und uff der statt viel er her ab und
zersprang in vier stuk. Do hiess der keiser Nero
die guotten herren sant Petter und sant Palum vachen und hiess si binden und hiess des zoubere<r>s
lip behalten, und wand, er sölt erstan an dem dri-
190   ten tag. Do sprach sant Petter, "Du solt wissen, keiser,

99. en

ought not go up to heaven from among the sinners. The Emperor Nero then ordered that they build for him a high tower, from which he would go up to heaven. When the (160) tower was made, all the people from Rome came there to watch. And Simon came wearing a crown and went up the tower and began to fly and the devils led him up into the air.

Then the emperor said to the apostles, "You have been defeated; don't you see (165) how he's going up into heaven?" Saint Peter then said, "Now let's wait awhile, so you will see that we are right and everything that he does, he does with the devil's help."

Nero then said, "You still stick to your belief. Don't you see (170) where he's going?" Then Saint Peter looked at Saint Paul. "Paul," he said, "look at Simon." Then Saint Paul raised his head and looked, and saw the sorcerer, and saw him flying.

He then said to Saint Peter, "Peter, for whom are you waiting, why don't you do (175) what you want to do?" Then the emperor heard what they were saying to each other and laughed and said, "They saw this, namely that they have been defeated, and now they're beginning to act like fools." Saint Peter then said to the emperor, "Now you will see that we aren't fools." Then Saint Paul said (180) to Saint Peter, "Do what you want to do immediately."

Then Saint Peter looked up towards Simon and said, "I order you devils, who are leading the sorcerer, who deceived many people, by oath in God's name that you let him fall and, from this time on, (185) lead him no more."

And immediately he fell down and broke into four pieces. The Emperor Nero then had the good Saint Peter and Saint Paul seized and ordered them bound and ordered the sorcerer's body to be preserved, believing he would arise on the third (190) day.[45] Then Saint Peter said, "You should know, Emperor,

44. literally 'broke'
45. i.e., it should not be buried

das *diser[100] zouber<er> nit mag erstan, wan er ist tot
des ewigen dotes." Do namen des keisers knecht
und viengen sant Pettern und sant Palum und
bunden si mit kettennen und leitten si in einen
195   kerker und kestgeten si dar in<u>n</u> nûn maunet. Do eins
tags ward, do gieng sant Petter usser dem kerker,   (p. 398)
und bekam im ûnser herr. Do fragt in sant Petter,
war er welte. Do sprach ûnser herr, er welte aber
gan gen Rom und gecrûtzget werden. Do gieng
200   sant Petter wider in und wart an einem crût-
ze gemartret und batt, das man im die füss uf
kerte an dem crûtz, und das houpt nider. Also
wart der himelfûrst gemartret und gap sin
lip und sin leben durch gott. Des selben tags wart
205   ouch dem guotten herren sant Palus sin houp<t> ab
geschlagen; und flos von siner kelen milch und
bluot, wan durch sin kelen gieng stetenklich süse ler.
Dar nach ward Nero, der keiser, schamlich von Rom
und vom dem rich vertriben und muost sich verbe-
210   rgen in den velsen, als ein wolf. Also sint dise grossen helgen ze himel komen hût und gevarn. Nun
biten wir gott, das si ûns helffen, das wir ouch
dar komen, da si sint. Des helff ûns gott, amen. It<u>em</u>.[101]

---

100. disen
101. It<u>em</u>. This word may indicate that another sermon or a sermon on another
feast after June 29, but before July 22, the date of the next feast (St. Mary Magdalene)
in the Rheinau collection, was to follow; this text may have been in the exemplar of
our copy.

that this sorcerer cannot arise, because he is dead forever."
Then the emperor's servants took and seized Saint Peter and
Saint Paul, and bound them with chains and led them into a
(195) prison, and maltreated them in there for nine months.

Then one day Saint Peter went out of the prison, and
our Lord came to him. Then Saint Peter asked him, where he
wanted to go. Then our Lord said, he wanted to go to Rome
again and be crucified. Saint Peter then went (200) back to
prison again, and he was martyred on a cross, and asked them
to turn his feet upward on the cross, and his head downward.
Thus the prince of heaven was martyred, and gave his body
and his life for God's sake. On the same day (205) the good
lord Saint Paul was also beheaded, and from his throat flowed
milk and blood, for sweet teachings went continually through
his throat.

After that the Emperor Nero was shamefully driven
from Rome and the empire, and had to (210) hide himself in
the cliffs like a wolf. Thus these great saints went and came to
heaven today. Now let us ask God, that they may help us, that
we too come to the place where they are. May God help us
with that, amen.

An sant Maria Magdalenen tag, item: (p. 398)

Wir lessent, do gott die welt geschuof, das er si
gröslich ziert mit zweigerhant geziert. Und also
er die welt geziert und si erlucht liplich mit der sun-   (p. 399)
5   en und mit dem maun, also hett er geistlich alle
menschlichen hertzen geziert und erlûcht mit zwein
liechtern, das ist, mit zwein frouwen, die bed heissent Maria. Und da von han ich vor gesprochen, "*Fecit[102]

Gen. 1:3-5

deus *luminaria[103] ma[n]gna;" das ist als vil gesproch-
10   en, "Ûnser herr haut gemacht zwei grosse liechter":
das mer liecht, das es liecht gep dem tag, das min-
der, das es schinn in der nacht. Dise zwei grosse liecht
sint min frouw santa Maria und sant Mari<a> Magdalena. Das erst liecht ist min frouw sant Maria. Die
15   hatt gott geschaffen dar umb, das si ein liecht sig allen
den, die da sint in dem tag, das ist, die aun sûnd sint,
das si inen sige ein liecht und ein sunn und ein bilt,
als si ein bilt vorgetragen hap, das wir ir nach volgen, wan si ist ein[104] liecht und ein schin aller guoten
20   lûtten, die da sint bezeichnet bi dem tag. Bi dem
minren liecht, das gott ouch geschuof, das es in der
nacht schinne, bi dem ist bezeichnet min frouw sant
Maria Magdalena, die da was ein liecht, das liecht ist aller sûnder. Wan bi dem sûnder ist bezeich-
25   net die nacht; wan als der mensch nit mag gesechen von der vinsteri, also mag der sûnder nit   (p. 400)
werden gesehen von gott, der da ist in der
nacht der vinstern sûnd. Und als die nacht
vinster ist und schwartz, also ist der sûnder
30   vinster und schwartz. Und da von spricht gott

102. fetit
103. lumiuariga
104. illegible letter attached to end of ein, marked out

On Saint Mary Magdalene's Day, another sermon:

We read that, when God created the world, he greatly adorned it with two kinds of adornment. And as he adorned the world and adorned it physically with the sun (5) and the moon, so he spiritually adorned and illuminated all human hearts with two lights, that is with two ladies, who both are named Mary. And for this reason I previously said, "Fecit deus luminaria magna;" that means as much (10) as, "Our Lord made two great lights," the greater light, that may give light to the day, the lesser, that it may shine in the night. These two great lights are my lady Saint Mary and Saint Mary Magdalene.

The first light is my lady Saint Mary. (15) God created her for the purpose that she may be a light to all those who are in the day, that is, those who are without sin, that she may be a light to them and a sun and an example, as if she had carried in front of us the example so that we may imitate it, for she is a light and a radiance for all good (20) people, who are signified by the day; with the lesser light, which God also created that it may shine in the night, is symbolized my lady Saint

Mary Magdalene, who was a light that is a light for all sinners. For the sinner represents (25) the night; for as a person cannot see because of darkness, so the sinner, who lives in the night of dark sin, cannot be seen by God.

And as the night is dark and black, so is the sinner (30) dark and black. And this is why God speaks

133

durch des wisagen munt, "Din antlit ist schwa-   Lam. 4:8
rtz worden als der schwartz kol," recht als ob
er spreche, "Din sel ist von sûnden schwartz worden als der schwartz kol." Da von haut ûns gott

35   hûtt fûr geleit einen biltner und ein sunen, das
wir, die da sûnder sigent, das wir bi ir nement
ein bischaft, also si sich von den sûnden schied, das
wir ûns ouch also da von scheiden; und also si ir sûnt
rûwet, das wir ouch also ûns lassen ûnser sûnde

40   rûwen. Wir lessent das santa Mariga Magdalena
und Marta und Laserus, das si drû warent gesch-
wist[g]erget. Nun wart sant Marigen Magdalenen ein man geben in ein statt, die hiess Magdalen. Si tett als menge leider hett getan und lûff

45   von dem man und kam gen Ierusolem und vergass ir eren und ir sel und ir erbern frûnden
und wart in der statt ein offne sûnderin. Wan
wir lesent, das si *besessen[105] was mit sûben tûflen,   (p. 401)
wan si gevallen was in sûben houptsûnd. Und nam

50   si ir schwester santa Martha und fuort si zuo einem
maul zuo ûnserm herren, und ver treip der die
tûfel von ir, und ward die sûnt hassent und lebt
dar nach selklich bi ir schwester Marthen. Do
ze einem mal ward, do war ein glichsner, der   Luke 7:56

55   batt ûnsern herren Iesum Cristum, das er mit
im esse. Das tett ûnser herr und gieng mit im und
sas nider. Do kam sant Maria Magdalena, die
was ein offin sûnderin gesin, und bracht ein bûchs-   Luke 7:37
sen mit salben und stuond hinder gott nach bi sin-   Luke 7:38

60   en füssen und begund ûnsers herren füss weschen
mit iren trechnen und trûchnen mit irem haur
und kust ûnserm herren sin götlichen füss und
salbet im si mit ir salben, die si dar hatt braucht.
Do dis der glichsner ersach, der in hatt geladen,

65   der gedacht in im selben, und wer dire ein wissag,   Luke 7:39

105. bessesen

through the prophet's mouth, "Your face has become as black as black coal," just as if he were saying, "Your soul has become as black from sins as black coal."

Accordingly, God has (35) set up before us a model and a sun, that we, who are sinners, take an example from her, as she separated herself from sins, that we too do the same; and as she repented of her sins, that we also allow ourselves (40) to be sorry for our sins.

We read that Saint Mary Magdalene, Martha, and Lazarus were siblings. Now, to Mary Magdalene a husband was given in a city which was called Magdalen. Unfortunately, she did what many have done, and ran away (45) from the man, and came to Jerusalem and forgot her honor and her soul and her honorable friends, and became a public sinner in the city. For we read that she was possessed by seven demons, because she had fallen into seven cardinal sins.

And one time (50) her sister Saint Martha took her to our Lord, and he expelled the demons from her. And she began to hate sin, and lived thereafter blissfully with her sister Martha.

Then it once happened that there was a Pharisee,[46] who (55) asked our Lord Jesus Christ to eat with him. Our Lord did that and went with him and sat down. Then Saint Mary Magdalene came, who was a public sinner, and brought a box with ointment and stood behind God near his (60) feet and began to wash our Lord's feet with her tears and dry them with her hair and kissed our Lord's divine feet and anointed them with her salve which she had brought along. When the Pharisee, who invited him, saw that, (65) he thought to himself, if he were a prophet,

---

46. The term 'glichsner' in the German text, translated here as 'Pharisee,' literally means 'hypocrite,' also 'double-dealer.'

so wiste er wol, wer dise wer, wan si ist ein
sûnderin. Do antwirt ûnser herr Simon, dem *glichs-   Luke 7:40
ner,[106] und sprach zuo im, "Simon, ich han mit dir
etwas ze reden." Do sprach Simon, der *glichsner,[107] un<u>d</u>

70   sprach, "*Meister,[108] nu sag, was du wellest." Do   (p. 402)
sprach ûnser herr zuo im, "Es was zuo einem   Luke 7:41
mal ein verkerer, dem sollten zwen man gel-
ten, und solt im einer v hundert pfenning,
der ander solt im l pfening. Dis hatten nit,   Luke 7:42

75   das si im möchten vergelten, und lies in
der verkerer beden die gûlt ab. Nun sag an,
Simon," sprach ûnser herr, "weder sol im billich-
er holt sin?" Do sprach Simon, "Der im de<ste>r hölder
Luke 7:43

*sölt[109] sin, dem er die meren gûlt ab gelassen

80   het." Do sprach ûnser herr zuo sant Marigen   Luke 7:43
Magdalenen und sprach ouch zuo Simon, "Sichstu
dise frouwen? Ich bin in din hus gegangen. Du
gebt minen füssen nit wasser, aber dise frouw
hatt sich nie uff, wan si wüsch mir min füsse

85   mit iren trechnen und wust mir si mit ir<u>em</u>
har. Du kustest mich nie, sit ich in din hus ka<u>m</u>,   Luke 7:45
si liess aber nit, si kust mir min füss. Du salbet-   Luke 7:46
test mir min houpt nit mit öl, aber dise frouw
hett mir minen lip gesalbet mit einer salben.

90   Und da von sag ich dir fûr war, ir ist vil sûnt   Luke 7:47
vergeben, wan si vil minn haut. Wan dem
man minre schult laut, der min<n>et dester min-   (p. 403)
der." Und do er mit Simem dem glichsner hatt
geredet, do sprach er zuo sant Marigen Magda-   Luke 7:48

95   lenen, "Frouw, ich vergeb dir din sûnd." Und die da
*sassen[110] bi inen, die sprachen, "Wer ist diser, der   Luke 7:49

106. verkerer
107. verkerer
108. meistur
109. selt with superscript o over e
110. ssasen

he would surely know who she was, for she is a sinner.

Then our Lord answered Simon, the Pharisee, and said to him, "Simon, I have something to talk about with you." Simon the Pharisee then spoke and (70) said, "Master, now tell me what you want."

Then our Lord said to him, "There was once a usurer, to whom two men owed money, and one owed him five hundred silver coins and the other one fifty.[47] They didn't have enough (75) to repay him, and the creditor released both of them from their debts. "Now tell me, Simon," said our Lord, "Which one should be more reasonably dear to him?" Simon then said, "He should be more dear to him, for whom he cancelled the greater debt."

(80) Our Lord then said to Saint Mary Magdalene and also said to Simon, "Do you see this woman? I came into your house. You gave no water for my feet, but this woman never hesitated to wash my feet (85) with her tears and wipe them with her hair. You never kissed me since I came into your house, but she hasn't stopped kissing my feet. You didn't anoint my head with oil, but this woman anointed my body with an ointment. (90) And, in truth, I tell you, many sins have been forgiven her, because she has great love. For the person whose lesser debt one cancels, he loves the less."

And when he had spoken with Simon the Pharisee, he said to Saint Mary (95) Magdalene, "Woman, I forgive you your sins." And those who sat with them said, "Who is this man who

47. The term used in the German text, 'pfenning' = Latin denarius.

den lûtten ir sûnt vergit?" Do sprach ûnser herr
zuo der frouwen und sprach, "Din geloup hat dich   Luke 7:50
behalten, gang in gottes frit." Von diser guote̱n
100   frouwen sant Marigen Magdalenen lessen wir,
do ûnser herr an dem crûtz hieng und all sin
iunger von vorchten von im fluchen, do stuont
si da unerschrokenlich bi dem crûtz und gieng
zuo dem grap, da er was gelegen. Und dar u[i]ber
105   ward si wirdig, das si den engel sach, der des
helgen grabes huot. Si was ouch das erst mensch,
das gott nach siner urstende sach. Wir lessent
ouch von ir, das si was bi den zwölfbotten, do si
entpfiengen den helgen geist und enpfieng
110   si mit inen, und das si niemen me wolt an-
sechen von dem grossen iamer und von der grossen liebe, so si zuo gott hatt. Und fuor von der welt
in ein wiesti und was da von der lûten geselschaft xl iare. Und do si als lang was gesin   (p. 404)
115   in der wüste aun allen trost, so die welt ge-
haben mag, und si niemen da wist wan gott
allein, do fuogt sich, das ein priester in die
wiesti kam in der meinung, das er gern
hett gesechen guot lût. Und kam an die statt,
120   da si was, und fragt si, wer si wer. Do sprach
si, si wer Maria, die offen sûnderin, und hett
in gott dar gesendet, das er si begrüp. Und also
do schied si von diser welt, der si lang gehass
was gesin. Und fuorten si die helgen engel
125   mit schönem gesang in das ewig himelrich
zuo gott, den si minnet vor allem und ûber
alle ding, der ir ouch hatt vergeben gross sûnd. Dis ist kurtzlich geseit von der helgen
frouwen sant Marigen Magdalenen. Da
130   von söllent wir sechen, wie wir ûnser leben an dire welt an vachen, wan dar um
ist ûns vor geschriben der helgen leben

forgives people their sins?" Our Lord then spoke to the woman and said, "Your faith has saved you, go in God's peace."

About this good (100) lady Saint Mary Magdalene we read that, when our Lord hung on the cross and all his disciples fled from him in fear, she stood there undauntedly at the cross, and went to the grave where he was laid. Because of this, she (105) became worthy of seeing the angel, who stood watch over the holy grave. She was also the first person whom God saw after his resurrection. We also read of her that she was with the apostles, when they received the Holy Spirit, and she received (110) him with them, and that she didn't want to see anyone anymore because of the great yearning[48] she suffered and the great love which she had for God. And she departed from the world into the desert, and was there separated from the companionship of human beings for forty years.

And when she had been (115) for such a long period in the desert without all the comfort which the world may have, and nobody knew that she was there except God alone, it happened that a priest came into the desert, as he liked to see devout people. And he came (120) to the place where she was, and asked her who she was. She said she was Mary, the public sinner, and that God had sent him there to bury her.

And thus she departed from this world which she had hated for a long time. And the holy angels led her (125) with beautiful singing into the eternal kingdom of heaven to God, whom she loved more than everything else, who also had forgiven her great sins.

This is briefly said about the holy lady Saint Mary Magdalene. Accordingly, (130) we should look to how we deal with our lives in this world, since for this purpose the lives of the saints are written for us,

---

48. in the sense of English 'pining, empathy'

und ir sûntliches leben, da si inn warent
vervallen, und ouch ir rûw, wie si wider
135   kamen zuo gottes hult—als, ob wir in sûnden sige<u>n</u>   (p. 405)
gevallen, das wir ouch mit inen mit rechter rû-
we wider erstanden. Nun sint wir leider also krank, das wir inen me volgent mit dem val in
die sûnd wan mit dem rûwen und mit der buos
140   von der sûnd. Und ist es, das wir untz her sint in
den sûnden gesin und wider gottes willen habent
gelebt, so flissent ûns hûtt, das wir dise frouwen
habent zuo einem biltner an rechter rûw und bicht, und bitten si ûns helffen hût bitten got, das
145   er ûns vergep all ûnser sûnt. Des helff ûns gott.

as well as their lives in sin into which they had previously fallen, and also their repentance, namely how they (135) came back to God's love—as, in case we should have fallen into sin, that we too with them may rise from the dead in true repentance.

Now we are, unfortunately, so weak that we follow them more with falling into sin than by repenting sin and atoning (140) for it. And if it is the case that up until now we have been in sins, and have lived contrary to God's will, then let us do our best today that we have this lady as a model of true contrition and confession, and let us ask her to help us today to ask God to (145) forgive all our sins. May God help us with this.

I tem:[111] An ûnser frou-   (p. 421)
wen tag, als sie in dem himel enpfangen wart.

Wir sint hût begant ûnser lieben frouwen tag,
als si von dire welt schied, und si gott mit lip
5   und mit sel wolt zuo im nemen in das himelrich. Und wan si und got warent geeinbart,
also, das si warent ein materi, da von wer es   (p. 422)
unmuglich ze gloupen, das ir lip, von dem gott geborn ward nach der menscheit, das der in dem
10   ertrich sölt fulen, als eins anderen menschen
lip, der in den sûnden ward geborn—in den erb-
sûnden—und in den sûnden lebt. Und wan si so
gar aun sûnd was, und gott sin liplich natur von
ir genomen hat, da von wolt er sin muotter,
15   die also schiet von diser welt, nemen in sin ewig
fröt, als es billenlichen was. Si verschiet, das si
wonung hett bi irem kint. Und wan es also
unmuglich was und ist, das dehein mensch-
licher lip kam in das himelrich E nach dem iu<n>-
20   gsten tag, da von nam die engel wunder, wer
die wer, die mit so grosser fröt und wunn kem
in das himelrich mit liplicher nattur, und sp-
rach<en>, das ist gesprochen, "Wer ist dise, die da uff
vert von der wiesti diser welt und in der   Song of Songs 8:5
25   wollust schwept und geneigt ist uff ir ge-
mintes liep?" Si mocht<en> wol sprechen, "Wer ist dise?" Wan es spricht *ûnser[112] herr in dem ewengelium, das niemen *kumt[113] in den himel vor   (p. 423)

111. This sermon begins in midline immediately following the text of the previous sermon in the manuscript (St. Lawrence).
112. vinser
113. kunt

Another sermon: On our Lady's Day, as she was received into heaven.

We are celebrating today our dear Lady's day, as she departed from this world, and God wanted to take her to himself, with body (5) and with soul, into the kingdom of heaven. And since she and God were united, such that they were one being, that is why it would be impossible to believe that her body, from which God was born in human form, should decompose in the (10) earth in the same manner as the body of any other person, who was born in sins—in original sin—and lives in sins. And since she was so entirely without sin, and God had taken on his physical nature from her, for this reason he wanted to take his mother, (15) who thus departed from this world, into his eternal joy, as was appropriate. She left this world so that she might dwell with her child.

And since it was—and is—so impossible, that any human body would come into the kingdom of heaven until after the last (20) judgment, the angels asked themselves in astonishment, who she was who came with such great joy and delight into the kingdom of heaven with a physical nature, and they spoke these words, "Who is this woman who rises up from the desert of this world and hovers in (25) delight, and is bent over her beloved?" They had good reason to ask, "Who is this woman?" For our Lord says in the Gospel that no one comes into the kingdom of heaven

        dem iungsten tag mit menschlicher nature,   John 3:13

30   wan der, der von dem himelrich komen was, go-
        ttes sun Ie<u>su</u>s Chr<u>istu</u>s. Da von nam bilich wunder
        al<le>s himelsches her, wer si wer, der hochzit wir
        hût begangen, das wir von der gnad des ho-
        chzites werden gebessret an lip und ouch an

35   sel. Ist, das wir sölen betrachten nach dem hoch-
        zit, das wir es wirdenklich begangen—wan
        es spricht ein grosser lerer, "Wir sölent an der
        helgen tag drû ding betrachten und in ûn-
        serm hertzen han"—, so mugen wir gnad von got

40   enpfachen. "Zuo dem ersten, so sond wir gedenke<u>n</u>
        an das leben, das der helig hatt an diser welt,
        des tag wir denn begand; zuo dem anderen
        mal, was ûns den<u>n</u> der helig hilfet und mag
        getuon gegen got. Zuo dem iii[114] mal so sölent

45   wir ouch betrach<t>en ûnser krankheit und ûn-
        ser noturft, das wir wol bedurfen ir hilff,
        wan si gottes in himelrich frûnt sint und
        bi im sint." Nun sölent wir hût began <den tag> des [gr]
        *grösten[115] helgen, der ie geborn wart und gehelget (p. 424)

50   uff ertrich, ûnser frouwen sant Marigen, gottes
        muotter; die söllent wir hût nemen zuo einnem
        biltner und volgent ir hût und ziechent ûns
        nach irem leben als völlenklich, als ûns denn got
        gnad gep an den tugenden, so si uff ertrich u[i]ebt,

55   wan si ist ein spiegel alles tugenthaften lebens, un<u>d</u>
        sunderlich so ist si ein spiegel aller frouwen. Si was
        demuotig, wan wir lessent von ir, das si was kû-
        nges geschlecht, und do ir der engel kunt, das
        si *got[116] sölte schwanger werden, das si sprach, "Got,"

                                               Luke 1:48

60   sprach si, "der hett angesechen die demuot siner
        dirnen." Wan das sprechent die helgen, "Und wer <nit>

114. iii superscript over andern, which is marked out
115. first two letters of grösten extend into left-hand margin
116. göt

with a human nature before the last judgment, (30) with the exception of him who had come from heaven, God's son, Jesus Christ. That is why the entire heavenly host with reason asked themselves in astonishment who she was, whose feast we are celebrating today, that we are bettered by the grace of the feast in body and also in (35) soul.

If we shall strive, in accordance with this high feast, to celebrate it worthily—for a great teacher says, "We shall on the feasts of the saints consider and have in our hearts three things"—then we can (40) receive grace from God. "First of all, we shall meditate on the life which the saint, whose day we are going to celebrate, had in this world; secondly, what the saint can do to help us, and can do before God. Thirdly, we shall (45) also think about our weakness and our need, namely that we surely need their help, for they are friends of God in heaven and are with him."

Now we shall celebrate today the feast of the greatest saint who was ever born and sanctified (50) on earth, our Lady, Saint Mary, God's mother; we shall take her today as a model, and follow her today and conduct ourselves in accordance with her life as completely as God gives us grace in the form of all the virtues which she practiced on earth. (55) For she is a mirror of all virtuous living, and especially, she is a model for all women.

She was humble, for we read of her, that she was of a royal family, and, when the angel announced to her that she would become pregnant with God, that she said, "God," (60) she said, "has seen the humility of his handmaiden." For the saints say, "If it weren't

Mariegen grosse demuot, si wer gottes muotter
nie worden." Wan wir finden, das vil megt ist
gesin, die vil gebetteten und gevasteten und ge-
65   wacheten und ouch demütig warent, aber so gros
und so volkomen demuot wart an frouwen lip
nie funden, sit das got den ersten menschen
geschuof. Und wan si als durnechtenklich
demütig was, da von wolt gott von ir gebor<u>n</u>
70   werden nach der menscheit, wan ûnser herr
E sprach und gesprochen het durch den wisage<u>n</u>
"Wa sol ich hin komen, da min gotheit rüw, wan   (p. 425)
in eins demütigen menschen hertzen?" *als[117] ob
er spreche, "Ich wil die menscheit von niemen
75   empfachen, noch geborn werden, denn von ei<u>m</u>
demütigen hertzen." Und wan demütiger me-
nsch nie geborn ward, da von wolt er nie geborn werden, *wa<u>n</u>[118] von einem demütigen menschen. Si was ouch[119] kûsches lebens, wan in der alten
80   E was gebotten, welle frouw nit kindete, das
die wer verflücht. Den fluoch nam si allen reine<u>n</u>,
kûschen frouwen ab, wan si was die erst, die ie
kûsches leben enthiess und *envieng.[120] Si wolt ouch
nit sin, da kein man hatt ze schaffen, und was ouch
85   nit vilredig[121] als vil frouwen, die man nun
fint. An diser tugent soltent all frouwen Marige<u>n</u>
nach volgen. Si mag wol han geredet, doch *vinde<u>n</u>[122]
wir nût in dem ewengelium von ir red den<u>n</u>
an drin stetten: Einest do si rett mit irm sun an
90   sant Johanes brutlouff, das selp mit kurtzen worden, do si sprach, "Si hant nit win." Da bi merkent   John 2:3
wir, das ein frouw nit reden sol, wan ir not-

117. und
118. we<u>n</u>
119. scribe originally wrote vch and corrected it to ouch
120. anvieng
121. horizontal line (hyphen?) between vil and redig
122. vinde<u>n</u> with ˆ over v

for Saint Mary's great humility, she would have never become God's mother." For we find that there have been many young women who prayed a lot and fasted and held (65) vigils and were also humble, but such great and perfect humility was never found in a woman's person since God created the first human being.

And since she was so completely humble, God wanted to be born of her (70) in human form, for our Lord said earlier and spoke through the prophet, "Where shall my divinity rest unless in the heart of a humble person?" as if he were saying, "I want (75) to be born from no one but from a humble heart." And because a more humble person was never born, he therefore never wanted to be born but from a humble person.

She was also characterized by a chaste life, for in the old law (80) it was established that whichever woman did not bear children would be cursed. She took this curse away from all pure, chaste women, for she was the first woman who ever promised a chaste life and yet conceived. She also didn't want to be where a man could do something with her, and also wasn't (85) talkative, as are many women one finds these days.[49]

As to this virtue, all women should imitate Saint Mary. She may well have talked, yet we find in the Gospel no more than three places where she speaks: Once she talked with her son at (90) the wedding of Saint John the Evangelist, even then with short words, as she said, "They don't have wine." Here we note that a woman shouldn't talk, except when it's necessary,

---

49. A euphemism probably referring to avoiding dangerous occasions or temptations to sins of the flesh.

durft, und das selp kurtzlich. So lessent wir zuo   Luke 1:26-38
dem andern mal, das si rett mit dem engel.   (p. 426)
95   Da bi merkent wir, das ein frouw mit fröm-
den mannen nit sol reden wan in der bicht,
wan bi dem engel ist bezeichnet der bichter.
So lessent wir zuom dritten mal, das si ouch ret
mit Elisabeth, ir muomen, sant Johanes des tou-   Luke 1:39-56
100   fers muoter. Da bi merken wir, das ein iunge
frouw mag reden mit einer witzigen und bi[d]-
derben frouwen, und ouch von witzigen und bi[d]-
derben dingen. Si kam ouch nie zuo iungen lûtten
an keinen spilhof. Da von, das si sich *vor[123] upikeit
105   behuot, da von ward si wirdig, das si gottes muotter ward. Es heisset wol der spilhoff, wan
da verspilet menge und menger sin sel und
lip. Da von fliechent den vnd gand in die kilchen
und redent da mit gott in ûwerm gebett, wan
110   also tett min frouw santa Maria. Da von ward
si gottes muotter. Zuo dem anderen mal soltu sunder ouch betrachten, das du ûnser frouwen
hilf wol bedarft von der krankheit der armen
welt, in der du bist, wan wir hand allsament
115   drig vigent, die ûns aun underlaus an vechtent: (p. 427)
den tûfel mit bösen retten vnd bösen geden-
ken, unsern lip mit bösen anvechtungen und mit
untugent. Und da von sont wir erkenen ûnser
notdurft und sond ûnser frouwen hût an rüffen
120   umb ir gnad, das si ûnser helferin in allen
ûnsern arbeitten also sige, wan wir sint krank
ze widerstand dem vigent und den sûnden,
und sint blöt, ûns ze *ûebent[124] an guotten werken.
Zuo dem dritten mal soltu betrachten die grossen
125   hilff, die si dir wil tuon, ob du si an rüfest mit
rechtem ernst, wan es spricht ein helg, Johanes

123. ver
124. ûebunt with superscript v over second u

and even then briefly. Secondly, we read that she spoke with the angel. (95) We note here that a woman shouldn't talk to strange men, except at confession, for by the angel the confessor is symbolized. And again we read as a third example, that she also talked with Elizabeth, her relative, (100) mother of Saint John the Baptist. We note here that a young woman can talk with a sensible and serious woman and also about sensible and serious matters.

She also never came to young people at any gaming hall. Because she guarded herself against frivolity, (105) she became worthy to become God's mother. It's well called a gaming hall, because there many women and men gamble away their soul and body. Therefore flee it and go to church and talk there with God in your prayer, for (110) thus did my Lady Saint Mary. That is why she became God's mother.

On the other hand you should consider that you very much need our Lady's help because of the weakness of the poor world in which you are, for we all together have (115) three enemies who unrelentingly assail us: the devil with evil advice and evil thoughts, our body with evil temptations, and with vice. And that is why we shall recognize our need and shall call upon our Lady today (120) for her grace, that she may thus be our helper in all our labors, for we are weak to withstand the enemy and sin, and are afraid to keep doing good works.

Thirdly, you should consider the great (125) help which she will provide you, if you call upon her with true sincerity, for a saint, John

Crisostiumus, "Also das unmuglich ist, das ûnser frouw dehein menschen ere, der ir nit von
allem hertzen getrûwet, also unmuglich ist, das
130   si deheim menschen versag, das si anrüffet
mit gantzer begirt sins hertzen und zuoversicht." Da von rüffent si hûtt an, wan si het hochzit mit ir kint und mit den englen in dem himelrich mit lip und mit sel und ist vol gnade<u>n</u>
135   und mag dir hût nit versagen. Und mag ir
ouch gott nit versagen, wan es spricht sant Ber<u>n</u>-   (p. 428)
hart, das spricht, "Du hest einen sichern zuogang
zuo gott. War umb? Du hast die muoter, Marige<u>n</u>,
vor irem kint ze fûrsprechen, die das kint fûr
140   dich bitt, und hastu das kint, das bit den vatter
fûr dich." Maria, gottes muotter, erzougt irem sun
die brûst, da mit si in sougt, und bittet fûr den sûnder. So zougt der sun dem vatter die wunden,
die er hatt gelitten mit siner gehorsame umb
145   die sûnder. Da von so ist unmuglich, so söliche
zeichen der almechtig gott sicht, er well sin
muotter eren umb den sûnder. Bittent si hûtt
umb ûwer noturft und grüssent si mit dem
Ave Maria. Land ûch nit erschreken, sigent ir in
150   sûnden. Si wer nie gottes muotter worden, und
werent <nit> sûnder; und wan si die er hatt von dem
sûnder, da von sol si bilich fûr den sûnder bitten,
von *dem[125] si so gross er haut, und ouch wan si ist vol
gnaden, wan was vol ist, das gaut gern ûber
155   und ist schûtig. Also sprich ich von ûnser frouwe<u>n</u>,
die ist vol gnaden. Si ist schûtig, wan der engel   Luke 1:28
sprach zuo ir, "Ave Maria, *gratia[126] plena, got grüs   (p. 429)
dich, vol gnaden." Si hat iren namen wol erfûlet
mit den werken, won si ist also gnaden rich,
160   das si ir genad also völenklich het[127] geteilt mit

125. den
126. gratzius
127. a spot of spilled ink covers nearly the entire word

Chrysostom, says, "As it is impossible (130) that our Lady honor any person who doesn't trust her with all his heart, so impossible is it that she refuse a person who calls upon her with all the desire of his heart and with confidence." Therefore let us call upon her today, for she celebrates with her child and the angels in the kingdom of heaven with body and with soul, and is full of grace, and (135) can't deny you anything today.

And God also can't refuse her. For Saint Bernard speaks, saying, "You have a sure access to God. Why? You have the mother as an advocate before her child, who pleads to the child for (140) you, and you have the child, who pleads to the Father for you."

Mary, God's mother, showed her son her breasts in order to suckle him, and intercedes for the sinner. Thus the Son showed the Father the wounds, which he suffered in his obedience for the sake of (145) the sinners. That is why it is impossible that, when almighty God sees such signs, he wouldn't want to honor his mother for the sinner's sake.

Plead to her today concerning your need and greet her with the Ave Maria. Don't let yourself be frightened, if you should be in (150) sins. She would have never become God's mother if there were no sinners; and because she has this honor from the sinner, she shall rightfully intercede for the sinner, from whom she has such great honor, and also because she is full of grace, for whatever is full, that gladly flows (155) and spills over. Thus I speak of our Lady, who is full of grace. She spills over, because the angel said to her, "Ave Maria, gratia plena, may God greet you, full of grace." She has truly fulfilled her name with her works, for she is so rich in grace, (160) that she so completely has shared her grace with

guotten lûtten und ouch mit sûndern, das si bilich wirt von iungen und von alten, von guotte<u>n</u>
und von sûndern gelopt. Und dar umb, das enkei<u>n</u>
mensch erschrek, wie sûndig es sige, es rüff si an,
165   dar umb so wil ich ûch ein bispel sagen und da
mit ein end. Wir lessent von einem pfaffen, der
hiess Theophelius, der was bi einem bischof und
hatt des gewalt allensament und hielt sich
dar an als wol und als götlich mit allen guote<u>n</u>
170   werken, das menglich wol gefiel. Do fuogt
es sich, das der bischof starb, bi dem er was, un<u>d</u>
ward Theophelius erwelt zuo einem bischof von
pfafen und von leigen, die er versprach von
grosser demuot, und wolt nit bischof werden.
175   Und ward da ein ander bischof gesetzt, und der
verstiess Theophelius von sinem gewalt. Do
fuor der bös kûndig tûfel zuo und benidet de<u>n</u>
bider man sins helgen und erberen lebens,   (p. 430)
und sant im bös gedenk in sin hertz und be-
180   gand im schwer machen, das er von so grossen
eren und gewalt verstossen was. Und gieng
Theophelius zuo einem zouberer, der was ein
iud, und batt den, das er im riete und ouch
hulfe, das er wider kem an sin er und an si-
185   nen gewalt. Der iud gap im einen brief, da
mit er den tûfel zuo im beschwör. Und kam
der tûfel und sach in Theophilius sitzen her-
lich uff einem stuol als einen kûng und gekrönt. Und stuonden ander tûfel fil da, als si wer-
190   ent sin ritter, und was vil liechter umb in.
Und der tûfel ret mit Theophilius und sprach,
wölt er gottes verlögnen und siner muotter
Marigen und aller ir hilf, und welt im des
brief gen, die mit sinem insigel werent besch-
195   lossen, so wölt er im helffen wider an sin er.
Das dett der arm Theophilius: Er schreib an ei-

good people and also with sinners, that she is rightfully
praised by young and by old, by good people and by sinners.

And in order that no one be afraid to call upon
her, however sinful he may be, (165) I want to tell you an
exemplum, and with that a morale.

We read about a cleric named Theophilus, who was
with a bishop and had his authority together with him, and
conducted himself in this respect so well and so devoutly with
good (170) works that it pleased many. Then it happened
that the bishop, with whom he was, died, and Theophilus
was chosen to be bishop by clergy and lay people, which he
declined out of great humility, and didn't want to become
bishop.

(175) And another bishop was appointed there, and
he deposed Theophilus from his authority. Then the evil and
crafty devil came and was jealous of the honest man's holy
and honorable life and he sent evil thoughts into his heart and
(180) began to make it hard for him to have been deposed
from such great honor and authority.

And Theophilus went to a sorcerer, who was a Jew,
and asked him to advise and also help him that he could
regain his honor and his (185) authority. The Jew gave him
a letter with which he could conjure up the devil to come to
him.

And the devil came and Theophilus saw him sitting
magnificently on a chair like a king and crowned. And many
other devils stood there, as if they (190) were his knights, and
there were many lights around him. And the devil talked to
Theophilus, saying, that if he wanted to deny God and his
mother Mary and all her aid, and if he wanted to give him
written evidence of this and (195) sealed with his seal, he
would help him regain his honor.

Poor Theophilus did that: He wrote in a

nen brief, das er verlögnete ûnser frouwen
und ir kindes, und das er von ir lip nit
wer geborn, und gap den brief dem tûfel,

200 und enpfieng in in sinen dienst. Do dis (p. 431)
was beschen, do fuogt es sich, das der bischof
all sin amptlût wandlet und sast Theophilius
wider an sin er und an sinen gewalt, und
ward als werd und als gewaltig, als er ie

205 was. Und do er etwe lang was an den eren
und in dem gewalt, do half im gott, das er
ze rûw kam, und gedacht in im selber, "Du weist nit, wenn du stirbest, hût oder morn. So muostu iemer me brinen in der hell umb din her-

210 schaft," und vorcht gott gar ser und stuond uff und
gieng in die kilchen. Und was dar inn fierzig
tag aun underlaus vnd vastet vnd bettet und
wachet aun underlaus. Und nam sin sûnd fûr
sich und gedacht, er wer unwirdig, das in got

215 erhorte umb sin sûnd; wan er sich hatt enzigen
gottes und siner muotter Marigen und er dar
über sinen brief und sin insigel hatt geben zuo
einer bestetung. Und do er lag in sölichen gedenken, do kam im ein zuoversicht in sin hertz, das

220 got niemen wölt verlorn lan werden, und bat
gott und ûnser frouwen, die da ist ein versünerin (p. 432)
des sûnders gegen dem almechtigen gott. Die stuont
bi im und trost in und seit im, das si im hult hett
gewunen um iren sun. Und do er si ersach und er-

225 hort, do erschrak er von fröden und was doch noch
vast beschwert dar umb, das er sin insigel und
sin hantveste dem tûfel hatt geben. Und leit sich
wider nider und weinet noch vester denn vor
und entschlief. Aber do kam ûnseri frouwen zuo im

230 und trost in aber und bracht den brief und hiess
in, das er sich frouwte und got lopte. Also erwachet
er und was fro und vand den brief uff siner

letter saying that he denied our Lady and her child, and that he wasn't born of her body, and he gave the letter to the devil, (200) and he received him into his service. After this had happened, it occurred that the bishop changed all of his officials and restored Theophilus to his honor and authority, and he became as worthy and powerful as he ever (205) was.

And when he for a certain length of time was in a state of honor and in power, God helped him come to repentance, and he thought to himself, "You don't know when you're going to die, today or tomorrow. So you'll have to burn evermore in hell because of your (210) high position gained with help from the devil." And he feared God quite sorely and stood up and went into the church. And he stayed there for forty days without interruption, fasting and praying and holding vigils unceasingly. And he put his sins in front of him and thought that he was not worthy that God would (215) hear him because of his sins; for he had given up God and his mother Mary, and had given his letter and his seal as a confirmation of that.

And when he lay there in such thoughts, a firm conviction came into his heart that (220) God didn't want to let anyone be lost, and he asked God and our Lady, who is a reconciler of the sinner with almighty God. She stood by him and consoled him and said to him, that she had gained favor for him with her son.

And when he saw her and heard her, he was startled with joy, and was yet heavily troubled, because he had given the devil his seal and handwritten confirmation. And he lay down again and wept even stronger than before and fell asleep.

Then our lady came to him again (230) and consoled him again and brought the letter and ordered him to rejoice and praise God. Thus he awoke and was happy and found the letter lying on his

brust ligen. Dar nach lept er untz an sinen dot in
gottes willen. Und do das zit kam, das er von [di]

235   diser welt scheiden muost, do enpfieng er ûnsern
herren und ward erlûcht als ein liecht und wart
got sechent von ougen zuo ougen und kam zuo got, da
er aun end iemer me fröt hett. <Bittent,> das wir nun also
hie geleben und die helgen also erent, das si gott

240   fûr ûns bitten und ûns umb got erwerben, das
wir niemer von in gescheiden werden, amen.

breast. From then on, he lived in God's will up until his death.

And when the time came that he had to depart from (235) this world, he received our Lord, and he was illuminated as a light and began to see God face to face and came to God, where he had evermore joy without end. Let us ask that we now may thus live here, and so honor the saints that they plead to God (240) for us, and for us from God obtain, that we are never separated from them, amen.

An aller helgen tag, it<u>em</u>: (p. 468)

Dise wort stant in dem ewengelium, das ma<u>n</u>
hût liset von allen helgen, der tag wir hût begant mit singen und mit lessen. Und spricht sant
5   Matteus also, "Des zittes, do ûnser herr uff ertrich
gieng, do sach er ein gross schar lûtten. Und do
er die lût sach, do gieng er sitzen uff einen be-   Matt. 5:1
rg und tett uff sinen götlichen mund und seit   Matt. 5:2
inen dise bredi und sprach also, 'Selig sint die   Matt. 5:3
10   armen des geistes, wan das himelrich ist ir,"   (p. 469)
recht als er spreche, 'Selig sint die, die da arm
sint des geistes der hochvart,' wan menger
mensch ist arm an dire welt, der ouch ewenklich
arm muos [muos] sin in ener welt, wan si haltent
15   sich in mengen weg als ûbel mit fluochen und
schelten, das in ir armuot wenig ze nutz *kumt[128] an ir
sel. Wir sechent mengen menschen, der arm ist,
das gott ût me erbût denn sin bok oder sin geisse,
wan das er also fûr sich hin lebt als ein ander vich:
20   Er stand uf, er gang nider, so gedenkt er niemer,
das er gott dank der gnaden, so er im teglich tuot,
mit einem patter noster. Und e er ein patter noster
spricht, er schwert e sûben stunt. Da wiss, als dik
du gottes namen verschwerest oder ûppenklich
25   nemest, es sig in zorn oder von gewonheit, das du
ûbergaust die zechen gebout, und als dik so du das
tuost, als dik tuostu totsûnd. Und wan du gott mit
schweren und mit andern sûnden verlûrest, [un<u>d</u>]
da von laut dich gott hie arm sin an dem guot un<u>d</u>
30   an ener welt an der sele <selig> iemer aun end. Disen
spricht gott nit, das si arm sigen und selig. Er spri-   (p. 470)
icht von den, das si selig sigen, die willenklich ar<u>m</u>

128. kunt

158

O n All Saints' Day, another sermon:

These words are written in the Gospel, which is read today about All Saints whose feast we are celebrating today with singing and with reading. And Saint (5) Matthew speaks as follows, "At the time at which our Lord walked upon the earth, he once saw a great group of people. And when he saw the people, he went to sit atop a mountain and opened his divine mouth and told them this sermon, speaking as follows, 'Blessed are the (10) poor in spirit, for theirs is the kingdom of heaven,'" just as if he had said, 'Blessed are those who are poor as to the spirit of pride,' for many a person is poor in this world, who also in eternity has to be poor in the other world, for they behave (15) themselves in many ways so badly with cursing and scolding, that their poverty avails them little in respect to their soul.

We see many a person who is poor, who offers God nothing but his billy goat or nanny goat, and thus lives on for himself as another animal: (20) Whether he stands up or lies down, he never considers thanking God with a Pater-noster for the grace He daily grants him. And before he recites a Pater-noster, he swears to God in vain seven times.

Be advised, as often as you swear in God's name in vain or insolently (25) use his name, be it in anger or out of habit, that you are transgressing the Ten Commandments, and as often as you do that, you are committing a deadly sin. And because you would lose God with swearing and other sins, that is why God lets you here be poor as to material wealth and (30) blessed in life eternal as to your soul forever without end.

To them God doesn't say that they should be poor and blessed. What he is saying about them is that they should be blessed who are willingly poor

sint und demütig und arm sint an hochvart, wa<u>n</u>
den armen hochvertigen hasset gott. Da von spricht

35   er, "Selig sint die armen des geistes, wan das him-   Matt. 5:3
elrich ist ir." Er spricht ouch zuo dem andern maul, "Se-

Matt. 5:5

lig sint die milten, wan si besitzen das ertrich der lebenden," das ist, si besitzent das himelrich mit lip und mit
sele. Die sint milt, die nût ûbel mit ûbel oder mit

40   wirsem geltent. "Selig sint, die da weinent, wan si wer-

Matt. 5:4

dent *getröstet."[129] Das sint die, die ir sûnt weine<u>n</u>t, nit
die da weinent, so si das guot verlierent oder die
frûnt; die sint nit selig, weder in dire welt noch
an ener welt. "Selig sint, die da hungeret vnd dûr-   Matt. 5:6

45   stet nach der gerechtikeit," der sich all zit ûebet an
der gerechtikeit, wan gerechtikeit ist ein tugent,
die einem ieklichen ding tuot, als es geordnet ist.
"Selig sint die erbarmhertzigen, wan gott wil   Matt. 5:7
sich an dem iungsten tag ûber si erbarmen." Nu<u>n</u>

50   sol ein *ieclich[130] mensch sich ûeben an erbermde
in drige wis: Bi dem ersten sol es sich erbarmen,
das gott so grosse martter haut erlitten durch
all der sûnder willen und noch hût lidet mit
der welt sûnd. Zuo dem andern maul erbarm

55   dich ûber din selbs sel, die in den sûnden ist, un<u>d</u>   (p. 471)
richt es darnach, das du nit verlorn werdest. Zuo
dem dritten maul, so erbarm dich ûber din [s] eben-
menschen, was im ûbel kum, das dir das leit
sige, und hilf im nach dinen statten mit wor-

60   tten und mit werken. So bistu selig und wil sich
gott ûber dich erbarmen an dem iungsten tag. "Se-
ligen sint die fridsamen," die frid hant von den   Matt. 5:9
sûnden und mit den lûtten, "die sint geheissen
gottes kint," wan got wil niena sin, denn da

129. getrötest
130. ietlich

and humble, and are poor as to haughtiness, for God hates
the poor person who is also haughty. That is why He (35)
says, "Blessed are the poor in spirit, for the kingdom of
heaven is theirs."

Secondly, he also says, "Blessed are the meek, for they
will own the earth of the living," that is, they will own the
kingdom of heaven with body and soul. Those are meek who
don't repay evil with evil or with something (40) worse.

"Blessed are those who weep, for they will be
consoled." They are those who bewail their sins, not those
who weep when they lose material wealth or friends; the latter
are neither blessed in this world nor in eternal life.

"Blessed are those who hunger and (45) thirst for
righteousness," that is he who practices righteousness all the
time, for righteousness is a virtue which deals with all beings
as they are ordered.

"Blessed are the merciful, for at the Last Judgment
God will be merciful upon them." Now (50) every single
person should cultivate mercy in three ways: First of all, he
should derive mercy from the fact that God has suffered such
a great martyrdom for the sake of all sinners and still suffers
today from the world's sins. Secondly, have mercy (55) with
your own soul, which is in sin, and take such care that you
don't become lost. Thirdly, have compassion with your fellow
man, whatever evil may befall him, that you are sorry for it,
and help him whenever you have an opportunity with words
(60) and with works. Thus you will be blessed and God will
have mercy on you at the Last Judgment.

"Blessed are the peaceful," that is those who have
peace with regard to their sins and are at peace with the
people, "they are called the children of God," for God doesn't
want to be anywhere except where there

65 frid ist. "Selig sint die, die da reines hertzen sint, Matt. 5:8
  wan die werdent gott sechent," wan enkein me-
  nsch, das in dotsûnden ist, das geschouwet got niemer, E es sin hertz von sûnden gerein<e>. "Selig sind,
  die da durechtung lident durch die gerechtikeit," Matt. 5:10
70 das ist, durch gott, der da ist die gerechtikeit, "das
  himelrich ist ir." Sint gedultig in ûwern arbeitten, in ûwer armuot, in ûwerm siechtagen; aun
  zwifel, gott wil mit ûch sin in ûwern arbeitten
  und in ûwer beschwerd. Es spricht *Davit[131] in dem
75 salter, "Mit dem menschen, der in beschwerd ist,
  mit dem bin ich in siner beschwerd." Und über Ps. 91:15
  das selb wort spricht der[132] *guot[133] sant Bernhard, "Herr
  gott von himel, sit du mit dem menschen wilt (p. 472)
  sin in siner beschwerd und in sinen arbeitten,
80 so bitt ich dich, das du mir arbeit niemer laussest
  gebresten an diser welt." Es spricht ouch sant Gregorius, "So ich sich und lis, das Job so gross arbeit
  und kumer hett, das er lip und guot und kint
  verlor, und sant Johanes, der nie sûnd get[t]et
85 und in siner muotter lip gehelget wart, das
  der so gross arbeit hatt, und das sant Petter, den
  gott also liep hatt, das er im enpfalch, ze enbinden und ze binden al<le>s, das wer in himelrich
  und uff ertrich, das er über den verhangt, das
90 er in als gross sûnd viel und das er wart er-
  henkt an das krûtz—da bi merk ich, her gott,
  das du din frûnd, die du liep hast und von dir selb
  hest erwelt in din rich, das du die last an vallen in dire welt not und liden." Da von sint die
95 selig, die durechtung lident an diser welt durch gottes willen und lident übel red, die man
  von in tuot. Gesach si gott, wan ir namen sint

131. davt, with superscript ^ over v
132. spricht der, der superscript
133. got with superscript v over o

(65) is peace.

"Blessed are those who are of a pure heart,
for they will see God," for no person will ever see God, unless
he first purifies his heart from sins.

"Blessed are those who suffer persecution for the
sake of righteousness," (70) that is, for God's sake, who is
righteousness, "the kingdom of heaven is theirs." Be patient
in your sorrows, in your poverty, in your illness; without a
doubt, God wants to be with you in your travails and in your
difficulties.

David says in the (75) Psalter, "With the person who
is in hardship, with him I am in his hardship." And about
these same words, good Saint Bernhard comments, "Lord
God from heaven, since you want to be with the person in
his affliction and in his hardships, (80) I ask you that you
never let me be without troubles in this world." Saint Gregory
also says,[50] "When I see and read that Job suffered such
great affliction and trouble that he lost body and property
and children, and that Saint John, who never committed a
sin (85) and was made holy in his mother's womb, was in
such great distress, and that God let it happen to Saint Peter,
whom He so loved that he commended him to unbind and to
bind everything in heaven and on earth, that He let it happen
to him that (90) he fell into such great sin, and that he was
hanged on the cross—from all of this I conclude, Lord God,
that you let fall upon your friends, whom you hold dear and
whom you for yourself chose to enter into your kingdom,
distress and suffering of this world." That is why those are
(95) blessed who suffer persecution in this world for God's
sake and suffer the slander that people inflict upon them.
Blessed are they,[51] for their names are

---

50. This quote, which seems to point to Gregory's Moralia in Iob, couldn't be
found in this extensive work. Perhaps it is more a paraphrase than a literal translation
of a quote.

51. 'Gesach si gott,' literally: 'God himself looked at them.'

geschriben in dem himelrich, und ir lon, der
ist gross vor gott. Dis ewengelium lessent wir
100   hût von allen helgen, und was die erste bredi
und die beste ler, die gott ie getett. Und wan
wir hût begangen aller helgen tag, da von   (p. 473)
merkent, wie sich dis helig hochzit huop und
wie es bi dem ersten anvieng, und war um.
105   Wir lesent also, das ze Rom was ein alter
tem<p>el,[134] der hiess Templum *Pantheon.[135] Das hatten
*ungloubig[136] lût gewicht in aller abgötten er. In de<u>n</u>
zitten was ein baubst, der hiess Bonifatzius. Der
verkert do die bössen gewonheit und wicht
110   das selb tempel in der ere ûnser frouwen sant
Marien. Und darnach ûber lang zit, do begond
sich die helig cristenheit meren und vast wa-
chsen. Und starb der bau<b>st Bonifa[n]tzius, und ward
ein ander gesetzt, der hiess Gregorius. Der satzt
115   und ordnet, das ma<u>n</u> d<u>az</u>[137] selb gotzhus wicht in der ere aller helgen, und tett das darum, wan sich die lût
dik in mengen weg versument an der helgen
tag durch das iar mit vasten und mit betten,
mit *viren,[138] und wie sich si versument, das si das
120   al<le>s sament hût bessrent und si sich mit inen ver-
sünent. Es ist hût ein grosser helgen tag. Da von
bittent all helgen umb ûwer noturft, wan
aun zwifel got mag innen nit versagen. Da
von bittent si, das si ûns umb gott erwerben   (p. 474)
125   ein leben, da mit wir behaltent sel und lip, amen.

---

134. temel, third stroke of m extended downward (beginning of p?), but
marked out
135. paucheon, with v (=u) over a
136. ungoulbig
137. ma<u>n</u> d<u>az</u> superscript over das selp
138. viren, with superscript ^ over v

written in the kingdom of heaven, and their reward is great
before God.

We read this Gospel (100) today about All Saints,
and it was the first sermon and the best teaching which God
ever did. And since we are celebrating today the day of all
saints, we should note how the feast originated and how it
began at first and why. (105) We read namely that there was
an old temple in Rome called the Templum Pantheon. Pagans
had dedicated it in honor of all the idols. At that time there
was a pope named Boniface. He then changed the evil custom
and dedicated (110) the temple in honor of our Lady Saint
Mary. And from then on for a long time, holy Christianity
began to increase and grow strongly.

And Pope Boniface died, and another was appointed
who was named Gregory. He established (115) and ordered
that the same House of God should be dedicated in honor
of all saints, and he did this because the people are often
negligent in many ways on the feasts of the saints throughout
the year about fasting and praying, even about celebrating
itself,[52] and so that, however neglectful they are, they make up
for all (120) this together today and reconcile themselves with
them.[53]

Today is a great saints' day. So let us pray to all the
saints for your needs, for without a doubt, God cannot say no
to them. For this reason let us ask them that they obtain for
us from God a kind of (125) life with which we preserve soul
and body, amen.

52. This probably refers to not coming to church to celebrate.
53. on the feast of All Saints

An aller sellen tag, it<u>em</u>:   (p. 474)

Dise wort stand geschriben in der epistel, die
man hût liset in der selmess, und schribt si
der guot santes Johanes in Apocolipsis. Und
5   wan wir gester in der helgen cristenheit be-
giengen aller helgen tag, da von haut die helig cristenheit geordnet und gesetzt, das
man hût begang aller selen tag, und als gester all helgen von der helgen cristenheit
10 wurdent gelopt und geeret, das also hût
all gloubig sellen wurden in dem vegfûr ge-
tröst. Und da von spricht der gut sant Johanes
"Selig sint die totten, die in gott," das ist, in gottes   Rev. 14:13
willen, "sterbent, wan der helig geist spricht, das
15 si nun ruowen von allen iren arbeitte<u>n</u>, wan ir
guotten werk, die volgent in nach." Nun lessent
wir von drigerleig tot, der die lût sterbent.
Der erst tot ist guot und nûtz, das ist, so der mensch die welt laut und alles das, das zerge-
20 nklich fröt git, und sich selber kestge[n]t durch
gott, und den sûnden stirbet, also das er kein
sûnd me tuot, die in von gott gescheiden mugen;   (p. 475)
der ist der welt tod und lebt gott. Des dodes helf
ûns allen gott, das wir den sûnden sterben. Sö-
25 lich totten bedurfent nit, das man fûr si bitte,
oder bett, oder vasste, wan si sint tot vo<u>n</u> aller not
und von aller arbeit. Der ander tot, des ouch die
lût sterbent, das ist so der mensch tuot ein totsûnt.
Von der sûnd wegen so stirbet der mensch an
30 der sele. Dissen tot sont wir alle fliechen, wan es
ist ein tot, da von lip und sel verdirbet und des
tûfels wirt. Gott beschirm ûns vor disem tod,
das wir des nit sterben. Und ververt der men-

O n All Souls' Day, another sermon:

These words are written in the Epistle which is read today in the Souls' Mass, and good Saint John writes them in the Apocalypse. And (5) because yesterday we in holy Christianity celebrated All Saints' Day, holy Christianity consequently ordered and established that we celebrate today All Souls' Day, and as yesterday all the saints of holy Christianity (10) were praised and honored, that thus today all the believing souls in purgatory should be consoled.

And good Saint John says concerning this, "Blessed are the dead, who die in God," that is, in God's will, "for the Holy Spirit says that (15) they now rest from all their afflictions; for their good works follow them."

Now we read of three kinds of deaths which people die. The first death is good and useful, that is, when a person leaves the world and everything which (20) gives transitory joy, and disciplines himself for God's sake, and dies to sins in such a way that he commits no more sins which can separate him from God; he is dead to the world and lives for God. With this death may God help us all, that we die to sins. (25) Such dead people have no need that people plead for them or pray or fast, since they are dead to all distress and to all affliction and to all pain.

The second death which the people also die, that is when the person commits a deadly sin. Because of the sin, the person dies (30) in his soul. We shall all flee this death, for it is a death because of which body and soul perish and become the property of the devil. May God shield us from this death, that we not die it.

And if the person

sch in einer totsûnt des willen oder werk, so ist
35   er ewenklich tot. Und verfacht in nit das gebett,
das man im nach tuot, und wirt beroubet aller der
gnaden, so die helig cristenheit tuot in aller welt,
das im sin niemer nût ze trost *kumt[139] alle die wil,
so er in den houptsûnden lebt aun rûw und bessrung.
40   Und wissent, wer sölichs tottes stirbet, das im nach
sinem tod niemen enkein guot nach sol tuon mit
almuossen, mit vasten, noch mit betten, wan es ist
im unnûtz. Der drit tod, der ist aller welt gemein,
guotten und bössen, iungen und alten. Dis dodes   (p. 476)
45   müssent wir alle sterben, und nach iekliches
werken wirt im gelonet. Haustu ûbel und sû-
ntlich gelebt, dar nach wirt dir gelonet. Hastu wol gelebt, so wirt dir wol gelonet. Und ist
das, das du grosse sûnd hast getan, bistu komen
50   ze rûw und ze bicht, so wirt dir nûtz alles, das
man dir nach tuot, wan du aun toudsûnd bist, und wirst
erlöst von dem fegfûr. Hast du aber niemen, der dir
sunderlich hilf tuot mit almuossen, mit messfrûm-
en und mit gebett, sich, so wirt dir diser hûtig tag
55   nûtz, wan so muostu wartten des gemeinen gebe-
ttes der helgen cristenheit. Und dar umb wart
diser hûtig tag uf gesest: Was die lût *versum-
tent[140] durch das iar an ir vorderen und allen
gloubigen sellen, das si das hût al<le>s erfûlent und
60   bessrent; und der niemen hetti, der *im[141] enkein
guot nach tetti, das dem hût wurd geholffen mit
dem gemeinen gebet der helgen cristenheit,
mit vassten, mit almuossen, mit opfer, die all
ein ieklich mensch sol tuon hût fûrderlicher den
65   zuo andern zitten. Des ersten tags, so der mensch stirbet, so sol man im oupfern dar umb, wan

139. kunt
140. versum-tint
141. in

goes astray, committing a deadly sin of will or deed, then he is (35) dead forever. And the prayer doesn't avail him which one says after him, and he is robbed of all the graces which holy Christianity grants them in all the world, so that nothing comes to console him during the whole time he lives in his cardinal sins without repentance and betterment. (40) And know that whoever dies such a death, after his death no one still needs do anything good for him with alms, with fasting, or with praying, for it is useless to him.

The third death is common to the entire world, good and evil, young and old. We must (45) all die this death and according to each one's works we are rewarded. If you have lived in evil and sin, you will be rewarded in kind. If you have lived well, you will be well rewarded. And if it is the case that you have committed great sins, and you have come (50) to repentance and to confession, then everything people do after you becomes useful to you, for you are without deadly sin, and you will be released from purgatory.

But if you have no one who can especially help you with alms, with benefits derived from Mass and with prayer, see, then this feast of today will become (55) useful to you, for in this way you have reason to look out for the common prayer of holy Christianity.

And for that reason the feast of this very day was established: Whatever the people neglected to do through the year for their forebears and all believing souls, that they accomplish that all and (60) better it, and if somebody should have no one who would do something good for him, that he is helped today with the common prayer of holy Christianity, with fasting, with alms, with offerings, all of which every person shall do today more promptly than (65) at other times.

The first day when a person dies, one shall make an offering for him, for

er den̲n̲ ist an der urteil gottes, weder er
zuo der hell söl oder zuo himel. Den sûbenden sol   (p. 477)
man dar umb begann, das im gott vergeb, wan
70   er sich gesumt hab an sinen zitten ûnsers herren,
die ein ieglich mensch von recht sol begann mit
gebett. Den dris[t]gesten sol man dar umb begann,
das im gott vergebe alles, das er ie getaun hap
wider gott in dem manet der drisig tagen. Das
75   iarzit begann wir dar umb, das innen gott vergep
alles, das si hand getan das gantz iar. Nun rüffen
wir gott an mit *gemeinem[142] gebet ûber alle
die sellen, der tag wir hût begand, das gott hût vergep
alles, das si wider in ie getatten und si zuo im neme
80   in das ewig rich und in die frout, die da niemer
zergaut. Des helf ûns got, der vatter, amen. It̲e̲m.[143]

142. gemeimem
143. It̲e̲m. This word may indicate that another sermon or item on All
Souls'Day or a sermon on another feast was to follow; this text may have been
in the exemplar of our copy.

he is then in the judgment of God as to whether he should go to hell or to heaven.

The seventh day[54] one shall celebrate with the hope that God may forgive him in case (70) he would have neglected to act during the times of our Lord,[55] which each and every person shall dutifully celebrate with prayer.

The thirtieth day one shall celebrate in hopes that God may forgive him for everything that he ever may have done against God in the month of thirty days.

The (75) anniversary we celebrate with the hope that God may forgive them everything they have done through the entire year.

Let us now call upon God in common prayer for all the souls whose feast we are celebrating today, so that God may forgive them today for everything which they ever did against him and may He bring them to Himself (80) into the eternal kingdom and into the joy that never ends. May God, the Father, help us with this, amen.

54. after a person is buried
55. This refers to (not) praying or attending Mass on the 'dies dominica' or Day of the Lord (Sunday).

An der helgen iunkfrouwen sant Katrien tag: (p. 482)

Dise wort stand geschriben in der Minne Buoch, und
spricht ûnser herr, "Du bist ein beschlosner gart, du

Song of Songs 4:12

bist ein gezierter brunn." Din usflus, das ist din
5   lere, und din wort und werk, das ist ein wolsmeken *des paradis.[144] Dis was die helig iunkfrouw santt
Katrina. Die was ein beschlossner gart gottes vor
aller bosheit und was ein gezierter brunn vor *allen[145]
untugen[t]den, und ir ler und ir guot bilt was ein
10   wolsmeken des *paradis.[146] Wan wir lessent von ir,
das si was eins kûnges dochter, der hiess Costus,
und was si gelert an allen kûnsten. Der selben zit
was ein keiser, der hiess Masentzius. Der besant
arm und rich in ein statt, die hiess Allexand[e]ria,
15   dar umb, das si den abgötten opfertin. Und die
es nit woltent tuon, die marteret er. Des zittes   (p. 483)
do was die helig iunkfrouw sant Kattrina uff ir
hus, wan ir was vatter und muotter tot, und richt si ir hus und gesint, wan si was gar rich und
20   was nit wan achzechen iar alt. Und do si das vich hort lügen, das man zuo treib, und es wolt opfern
den abgötten, do sant si einen botten, das er erfüre,
was es meinde oder was es wer. Und do si vernam
von dem botten, was es was, do nam si irs gesindes
25   etwie fil und macht das helig crûtz an ir hertz
und was gar leidig und beschwert, das man die
cristnen lût also zwang zuo dem uncristnen opfer.
Und gieng zuo dem keiser und sprach also, "Erkan-
destu dinen schöpfer und zugest din hertz von sö-

144. das
145. aller
146. baradis

On the holy virgin Saint Catherine's Day:

These words are written in the Book of Love, and our Lord says, "You are an enclosed garden, you are a decorated fountain." [56] What flows out of you are your (5) teachings. And your words and your works are a pleasant fragrance of paradise.

This was the holy virgin Saint Catherine. She was an enclosed garden of God, closed off from all evil, and was an adorned fountain, sealed against all vices, and her teachings and her good example were a (10) fragrance of paradise. For we read about her, that she was the daughter of a king who was named Costus, and she was instructed in all seven liberal arts.

At the same time, there was an emperor named Masencius. He sent poor and rich people to a city which was called Alexandria (15) in order that they would sacrifice to the idols. And those who didn't want to do it, he made suffer. At that time, the holy virgin Saint Catherine was at her house, for her father and mother were dead, and she managed her house and her servants, for she was quite rich and (20) was only eighteen years old. And when she heard the cattle lowing, which they drove closer and wanted to offer to the idols, she sent a messenger to find out what it meant or what it was.

Then she took (25) quite a lot of her servants and made the holy cross on her heart, and was quite downhearted and troubled that Christian people were forced in such a way to make the unchristian sacrifice. And she went to the emperor and spoke as follows, "If you acknowledged your Creator and withdrew your heart from such

---

56. This is the book of the Song of Songs, attributed to Solomon.

30   licher meintat, so werestu wirdig des gruosses. Und
      gedenk, weder gott gewaltiger sig oder die göt,
      die du anbettetest. Und wenn du in wirst erke-
      nnen, so vindestu im niemen gelich. Da von lop
      got und dien im, wan er ist ein herr ob allen he-
35   ren und ein gott ob allen götten." Und do si im vil
      vor geseit, do sprach der keisser, "Laus ûns dis opfer
      volbringen," und hiess si füren uff einen pfallentz,
      und kam do der keisser darnach und sprach
      zuo ir, "Wir hand din red wol gehört, und wundert (p. 484)
40   ûns diner wisheit. Sag ûns din geschlecht!" Do spra-
      ch sant Katrinna, "Ich bin Katrina, des kûngs Costus
      dochter. Und wie ich ward geborn und erzogen
      in pfeller und wie ich han gelernet die sûben
      kûnst, das versmachen ich alles sament und wil
45   gott nach volgen, wan din göt mogent niemen
      gehelffen, noch inen selber." Do sprach der keiser,
      "Nach diner red so irete alle die welt, und tetestu
      allein recht; wan werestu ein engel, ich sölte sö-
      lichen wortten nit glouben. Nun bistu ein wip." Do
50   sprach sant Katrina, "Nun zûrn nit, wan ist das, das
      du dinen zorn macht gerichten, so bistu ein kûng;
      machtu in nit gerichten, so bistu ein knecht." Do
      der keiser sach, das er ir wisheit nit mocht ge-
      antwirten, do sant er heimlich in alle lant nach
55   den besten meistern, das si kemen und die iunk-
      frouwen ûberwunden. Do wurden fûnfzig der
      besten meistern bracht, die das lant und all rich
      mochten geleisten. Und do si zuo im kament, do fr-
      agten si, was er wölt, das er si von so veren landen
60   het besant. Do sprach der keisser, "Hie ist ein tochter, die
      hett ûnser göt versmachet, und ist so kunstenrich, das

(30) a crime, you would be worthy of a friendly greeting. And consider whether God is more powerful than the gods you worshipped. And if you will acknowledge him, then you will find none equal to him. Therefore praise God and serve him, for he is a Lord above all (35) lords and a God above all gods."

And after she had said much to him in his presence, the emperor said, "Let us carry out this sacrifice," and had her led up to a palace. And the emperor came afterwards and said to her, "We have heard well your speech, and your wisdom (40) has amazed us. Tell us the family from which you come."

Then Saint Catherine said, "I am Catherine, King Costus' daughter. And as I was born and raised in sumptuous clothing, and although I learned the seven arts, I disdain all of that, and want to (45) follow God, for your gods can help no one, not even themselves."

The emperor then said, "According to your word, then, the entire world is in error, and you alone would be correct; even if you were an angel, I shouldn't believe such words. Now you are only a woman."

Then (50) Saint Catherine said, "Now don't grow angry, for only if you can control your anger, you are a king;[57] if you cannot control it, you are a slave."

When the emperor saw that he couldn't defend himself against her wisdom, he sent secretly into all the lands for (55) the best intellects,[58] inviting them to come and defeat the young woman. Then fifty of the best masters the country and the entire empire could supply were brought on.

And when they came to him, they asked what he wanted for having sent (60) for them from such distant lands. The emperor said, "There is a young lady[59] here who has

---

57. Literally, 'rule your anger.' In a play on words, the Latin 'rex'/'regere,' 'ruler'/'to rule' is behind the German kûng/gerichten.
58. literally, 'masters, teachers'
59. literally, 'daughter'

das unsaglich ist. Überwinde<u>nt</u> ir di, ich wil ûch
gross guot geben und wil ûch erhöchen in mine<u>m</u>   (p. 485)
rich." Do sprach ein meister, "Der minst, der under
65   ûns ist, der hett das ding wol us gericht. Doch heiss die tochter komen, das wir si richten von ir ir<r>et
und von ir torheit." Do man sant Katrinen dar bracht und sie die meister ersach, do macht si ein crûtz
fûr sich und enpfalch sich got. Und stuont ein eng-
70   el zuo ir und hiess si vest sin, wan si wurt die meister al ûberwinden. Sant Katrina kam fûr das
gericht, und kriegtent die meister vast wider si
umb den glouben. Und antwirt in sant Kattrin
so flissenklich, das si vor ir stuonden als stumen.
75   Do ward der keisser uff si zornig und sprach, wie
schamlich si sich liessen überwinden von einer
iungen tochter. Do sprach ir oberster meister,
der under innen was, "Wissest, keiser, das ûns
nie mensch mocht widerstan an kunst untz an
80   dise tochter, die ûns dar zuo haut bracht, das wir
ir wisheit nit kunen geantwirtten. Ouch du un-
derwisest ûns bas von den abgötten, die wir
untz her angebettet hant, wir[147] bekerent ûns
all zuo dem got, von dem si seit." Do der keiser das
85   erhort, do hiess er si all verbrenen in einem fûr;
do starkt si sant Kattrin an dem glouben. Und do   (p. 486)
man si in das fûr warf, do machtent si das
crûtz vor in und verschieden also, das ir haur
*noch[148] ir gewand nie versengt wart von dem
90   fûr. Und do man si begruop, do sprach der keiser, "Edli tochter, beraut dich, und volg ûns. Ich
wil, das du nach der keiserin die oberest sigest, und wil ein bilt nach dir machen, das
menglich an muoss betten." Do sprach die ma-

---

147. incomplete, semicircular letter between hant and wir
148. nach

disparaged our gods, and is so learned that
it boggles the mind. If you beat her, I will give you great
wealth and exalt you in my empire."

Then a master said, "The least (65) amongst us would
certainly have taken care of the matter. But let the young
lady[59] come that we direct her away from her erroneous
message and her foolishness."

When Saint Catherine was brought and she saw
the masters, she made the sign of a cross over herself and
commended herself to God. And an angel stood (70) with
her and ordered her to be strong, for she would defeat all the
masters. Saint Catherine came before the panel of scholars,
and the masters debated hotly against her about the faith.
And Saint Catherine answered them so conscientiously that
they stood before her dumbfounded.

(75) Then the emperor grew angry at them and said,
how shamefully they let themselves be defeated by a young
woman. Then the highest master among them said, "May
you know, emperor, that no one could defeat us in the arts
(80) until this young woman,[59] who brought us to the point
where we didn't know how to react to her wisdom. Unless
you instruct us more thoroughly about the gods we have
worshiped up until now, we are all going to convert to the
God she talks about."

When the emperor heard that, (85) he ordered that
they all be burned in a fire; at that time Saint Catherine
strengthened them in the faith. And when they were thrown
into the fire, they made the cross over themselves and thus
died in such a way that neither their hair nor their clothing
was ever singed by the (90) fire.[60] And when they buried
them, the emperor said, "Noble young lady,[59] think about
this and follow us. I want you to be the highest lady after
the empress, and I want to make a picture of you, which all
people will have to worship."

60. literally, 'departed'

95   gt, "Schwig! Wan es ist meintat ze gedenk-
ent, das du redest, wan ich mich selber gemechelt hab Je_su_s Chri_stu_s, der ist min minn,
der ist min zart, der ist min süsikeit, von
des liebi scheidet mich weder zartten

100   noch trouwen." Do hiess er si abziechen und
hiess si vast schlachen mit geislen und si fü-
ren in ein vinsteri und liess si da ligen zwe-
lff tag aun essen und aun trinken. Und wart
der keisser ritent dannen. Und kam die kei-

105   serin, und nam mit ir einen ritter, der hiess
Profirius, der was der gewaltiges<t> ritter,
den der keiser hatt, und gieng zuo sant Katrinen in den kerker. Und sachent si in [in] grosser
schöni und heitteri ligen und sache_n_t, das

110   der engel iren zerschlagenen lip salpte[n].[149] Do vieng   (p. 487)
an sant Katrin un_d_ seit inen von dem glouben un_d_
von der kristenheit und brediget inen untz zuo
miternacht. Do dis P<ro>firius der riter erhort, do
viel er in ze fuos mit zwein hundert rite<r>n und

115   enpfieng da cristnen glouben. Do kam got mit
sinen helgen englen und sprach zuo sant Katrin-
en, "Sich den herren, durch den du alles dis liden
hest gelitten, und bis vest an diner marter, wa_n_
ich wil mit dir sin." Do kam der keiser und hiess

120   si fûr in bringen. Und do er sach, das si schöner
was de_n_n vor, do wand er, man hette ir teglich
ze essen geben, und hiess die kestgen, die ir huoten.
Do sprach die magt, "Mir gap nie mensch ze ese_n_
wan gott von himel, der spist mich mit sine_n_

125   englen." Do sprach dire keiser aber, "Du erwel
under zwei dingen eins: Ei<n>tweder du opfer
ûnsern götten, oder du muost sterben eins iemer-
liches todes." Do sprach sant Katrin, "Marter mich

---

149. salpten, t superscript

The young woman then said,
(95) "Don't say that! For it's blasphemy to consider what
you're saying, for I've been given as a bride to Jesus Christ,
who is my love, who is my tenderness, who is my sweetness,
from whose love neither flattery (100) nor menace separate
me."

He then commanded to undress her and to beat her
hard with whips and to lead her into a dark place, and he
left her lying there for twelve days without food and without
drink. And the emperor rode forth from there.

And the (105) empress came and took with her a
knight named Profirius, who was the most powerful knight
the emperor had, and went into the prison to Saint Catherine.
And they saw her lying there in great beauty and serenity, and
saw that (110) the angel anointed her battered body. Saint
Catherine then began to tell them about the faith and about
Christianity, and preached to them up until midnight. When
the knight Profirius heard this, he fell at her feet with two
hundred knights and (115) received there the Christian faith.

Then God and his holy angels came and said to Saint
Catherine, "See the Lord, for whose sake you have suffered all
this pain, and be firm in your martyrdom, for I will be with
you." Then the emperor appeared and gave orders (120) to
bring her before him. And when he saw that she was more
beautiful than before, he presumed that they had given her
food to eat every day, and ordered those punished who were
guarding her.

Then the young woman said, "No one ever gave me
anything to eat except God from heaven, who with (125) his
angels nourished me."

But the emperor then said, "You choose one out of
two things! Either you sacrifice to our gods, or you will suffer
a miserable death."

    des iemerlichesten todes, so du kûnest erdenken!

130   Des wil ich wilenklich und frölich durch mins
    heren gotes, Jesus Christus, willen sterben, wan er ouch
    sich selben an den tod gap durch minen willen."   (p. 488)
    Do hiess der keiser machen vier reder und hies
    die fûllen scharpfer messer und hiess si dar in

135   sitzen, das si die reder alle[r] zerhûwen und das
    cristen lût da von erschreken. Do bat sant Katrin
    ûnsern herren, das er die reder liess brechen,
    im selber ze ere und andern lûtten ze besrung.
    Uff der statt zerbrachent die reder als unge-

140   hûrlichen, das si vier tusent heiden erschluogen.
    Und do die keiserin das ersach, do straft si den
    keiser umb sin grossen hertikeit, und wolt die
    keiserin den abgötten nit me opfren. Und do
    der keiser das ersach, do hiess er der keiserin ir

145   brûst ab winden und darnach ir houpt abschl-
    lachen. Und do si an die marter gieng, do bat
    si sant Katrinen, das si got fûr si bet. Do sprach
    sant Kattrina, "Fûrcht dir nit, wan dir wirt
    umb ein zergenklich leben geben das ewig

150   leben und das ewig rich." Und do si ent[t]houptet
    ward, do nam Proffirius der keiserin lip und
    begruop si. Und do der keiser fragt, wie der kei-
    serin lip wer beschen, oder wer si begrapen
    hett, do sprach P<ro>firius, "Ich han der keiserin

155   cristnen lip begrapen und han ouch cristnen   (p. 489)
    glouben enpfangen." Do schrei der keiser[150] <mit> einer grû-
    lichen stim, "Und sechent her, alle! Der mins lips huo-
    tter was, der ist verkert." Do sprach Profirius, "Ich bin
    nit verkert, ich bin bekert." Also sprachent ouch die

160   andern und sprachent, "Wir sint bereit ze sterben
    durch gott und durch cristnen glouben." Do hiess der
    keiser Profirius und die zwei hundert ritter

150. h and beginning of e written between der and keiser

Saint Catherine then said, "Make me suffer
the most miserable death that you can think up; (130) this
death I will willingly and cheerfully die for the sake of my
Lord God, Jesus Christ, for he also gave himself up to death
for my sake."

Then the emperor commanded four wheels to be
made and ordered them filled with sharp knives, and ordered
her to (135) sit therein, so that the wheels would chop her
totally to pieces and so that also the Christians would be
terrified by this.

Then Saint Catherine asked our Lord that he
would let all the wheels break, in his own honor and to the
betterment of other people. Immediately the wheels broke
into pieces so (140) frightfully that four thousand heathens
were killed.

And when the empress saw that, she reprimanded the
emperor for his great cruelty, and the empress didn't want to
sacrifice to the idols any more. And when the emperor saw
this, he ordered the empress's (145) breasts cut off and herself
thereafter to be beheaded.

And when she went to her martyrdom, she asked
Saint Catherine to pray to God on her behalf. Saint Catherine
then said, "Don't be afraid, instead of a transitory life you will
be given the eternal (150) life and the eternal kingdom."

And when she was beheaded, Profirius took the
empress's body and buried her. And when the emperor
asked, how the body of the empress was dealt with, or who
had buried her, Profirius said, "I buried the empress's (155)
Christian body, and I also received the Christian faith."

The emperor then cried out in a gruesome voice, "And
look here, everyone! He, who was my bodyguard, is perverted!"
Then Profirius said, "I am not perverted, I am converted."

The (160) others also spoke like this and said, "We are
ready to die for God's sake and for the sake of the Christian
faith."

Then the emperor commanded that Profirius and the

enthoupten. Do sprach sant Kattrin, "Tuo das du an
habest gevangen!" Und do si wart gefürt dar, da
165   man si solt enthoupten, do huop si ir hend uf ze himel und sprach, "Zuoversicht und heil aller gloupiger
cristner lûtten, Iesus Cristus, ich bit, wer minen
marterlichen tag begang oder an sinem tot mich
mit gantzem rûwen an rüff, oder in keiner siner
170   not, das du in erest und im helfest." Do kam ein stim
von himel und sprach, "Kum her, min geminte! Dir
ist der himel uf getan, und allen den, die dinen
tag begant, die wil ich aller dingen eren." Und
do si enthouptet ward, do flos von ir kelen milch
175   fûr das bluot, und kament die helgen engel und
fuortent iren lip ûber zwenzig tagweid *fer[151]
uff einen berg, der hiess Sina, und begruopen in da.
Und flûset da von ir lip und von ir gebein öl   (p. 490)
aun underlaus. Von dem öl meng siecher mensch
180   enpfachet gesuntheit sins lips, was siechtagen
der mensch hett. Nun bittent wir die guoten helgen iunkfrouwen sant Katrinan, das si hût und
alle zit gott fûr ûns well bitten, das er ûns durch irn willen und durch siner grossen erbermt
185   willen ûnser sûnd vergep und ûns die gnat
gebe, das wir ûns an dire armen welt also richten, das wir von der ewigen fröt niemer
werden verstossen. Des helff ûns allen der vatter und der sun und der helig geist, amen. Item.[152]

---

151. for
152. The sermon on Saint Catherine is the last one in the Rheinauer
Predigtsammlung manuscript. Following this sermon there are two lines in which
the scribe asks the readers, 'Bitent got fûr das dis geschriben hett, das im got helff
zuo eim guotten ent, item' = 'Pray to God for it who wrote this that God help him
toward a good end'. Apparently, this phrase is formulated neutrally as to gender, but
the German word 'im'(usually dative singular masculine = 'him') is likely to refer to
a male. The word 'item' = 'another piece or item' in l. 189 may well refer to these
lines.

two hundred knights
be beheaded. Saint Catherine then said, "Carry out what you began!"

And when she was led forth to where (165) she was to be executed, she raised her hands to heaven and said, "Oh hope and salvation for all believing Christians, Jesus Christ, I ask that, whoever celebrates the feast of my martyrdom or at his death calls upon me with total repentance or in any (170) need of his, you honor him and help him."

Then a voice came from heaven and said, "Come here, my beloved. Heaven is opened to you and to all those who celebrate your feast day, whom I want to honor in all things."

And when she was beheaded, milk flowed from her throat (175) instead of blood, and the holy angels came and carried her body over a distance of a twenty days' journey up to a mountain named Sinai and buried it there. And there flowed oil incessantly from her body and from her bones. From the oil many a person (180) received new health of his body, whatever illness the person had.

Let us now ask the good holy virgin Saint Catherine to plead for us before God today and at all times, that he may forgive us our sins for her (185) sake and for the sake of his great mercy, and give us the grace, that we direct our lives in this poor world so that we are never [61]expelled from eternal joy. May we be helped in all of this by the Father, the Son and the Holy Ghost, amen.

Selected Bibliography and Indices

Selected Bibliography

Bischoff, Bernhard. *Latin Palaeography. Antiquity and the Middle Ages.* Trans. Dáibhí Ó Cróinín and David Ganz. Cambridge: Cambridge University Press, 1990.

Bruckner, Albert. *Scriptoria medii aevi Helvetica: Denkmäler schweizerischer Schreibkunst des Mittelalters.* Geneva: Roto-Sadag, 1934-78. Vol. 4 (1940): *Schreibschulen der Diözese Konstanz: Stadt und Landschaft Zürich.*

Caesarius Heisterbacensis. *Dialogus Miraculorum.* Ed. Jos. Strange. 1851, rpt. Ridgewood, N.J.: Gregg, 1966.

Cruel, Rudolf. *Geschichte der deutschen Predigt im Mittelalter.* 1879, rpt. Hildesheim: Georg Olms Verlagsbuchhandlung, 1966.

Grässe, Th., ed. *Jacobi a Voragine Legenda Aurea: Vulgo Historia Lombardica Dicta.* 1890, rpt. Osnabrück: Zeller, 1969.

Hänggi, A., ed. *Der Rheinauer Liber Ordinarius (Zürich Rh 80, Anfang 12. Jh.).* Fribourg: Universitätsverlag, 1957.

Huber, Michael. "Homilienfragmente aus der Benediktinerstiftsbibliothek Metten." *Münchener Museum für Philologie des Mittelalters und der Renaissance* 1 (1911, rpt. 1972): 339-55.

Klapper, Joseph, ed. *Erzählungen des Mittelalters.* Volkskundliche Arbeiten namens der Schlesischen Gesellschaft für Volkskunde. Vol. 12. Breslau: Marcus, 1914.

Little, A.G. *Liber Exemplorum: ad usum praedicantium.* Vol. 1. British Society of Franciscan Studies. Aberdeen: Typis Academicis, 1908.

Mohlberg, Leo Cunibert. *Katalog der Handschriften der Zentralbibliothek Zürich.* Vol. l. Mittelalterliche Handschriften. Zürich: Buchdruckerei Berichthaus, 1952.

Oesterley, Hermann, ed. *Gesta Romanorum.* Berlin: Weidmannsche Buchhandlung, 1872.

Ryan, William Granger, trans. *Jacobus de Voragine: The Golden Legend. Readings on the Saints.* 2 vols. Princeton, N.J.: Princeton University Press, 1993.

Salzgeber, Joachim. "Rheinau." *Lexikon für Theologie und Kirche,* vol. 8: col. 1155-56. Freiburg: Herder, 1999.

Schiewer, Hans-Jochen. "Rheinauer Predigtsammlung." *Die deutsche Literatur des Mittelalters: Verfasserlexikon.* Ed. Kurt Ruh, et al., vol. 8: col. 28-31. Berlin: Walter de Gruyter, 1992.

Schneyer, Johann Baptist. *Geschichte der katholischen Predigt.* Freiburg: Seelsorge Verlag, 1969.

Trigonella, Francesca. "Ausgewählte Predigten aus der Handschrift C 102 a der Zentralbibliothek Zürich. Text und Kommentar." Lizentiatsarbeit, Universität Zürich, 1996.

Wackernagel, Wilhelm. *Altdeutsche Predigten und Gebete aus Handschriften.* 1876, rpt. Darmstadt: Wissenschaftliche Buchgesellschaft, 1964 (contains a survey, "Die altdeutsche Predigt": 291-445).

Wenzel, Siegfried. "The Three Enemies of Man." Mediaeval Studies 29 (1967): 47-66.

Werner, J. "Volkskundliches aus einer Rheinauer Predigtsammlung des 15. Jahrhunderts." *Schweizerisches Archiv für Volkskunde* 26 (1926): 280-92.

Wilkinson, James Chris. "De Sanctis: a Collection of Fifteenth Century Swiss Sermons in the Vernacular." Ph.D. diss., University of North Carolina at Chapel Hill, 1988.

Wolter, Eugen, ed. *Der Judenknabe: 5 griechische, 14 lateinische und 8 französische Texte.* Bibliotheca Normannica, vol. 2. Halle: Niemeyer, 1879.

Index

SCRIPTURE INDEX

191